What Do You Call Him?
Unveiling 160 Names of God

What Do You Call Him? Unveiling 160 Names of God

A Synopsis of God's Names through Biblical Accounts

Shavonne R. Ruffin

RESOURCE *Publications* • Eugene, Oregon

WHAT DO YOU CALL HIM? UNVEILING 160 NAMES OF GOD
A Synopsis of God's Names through Biblical Accounts

Copyright © 2021 Shavonne R. Ruffin. All rights reserved. Except for brief quotations in critical publications or reviews, no part of this book may be reproduced in any manner without prior written permission from the publisher. Write: Permissions, Wipf and Stock Publishers, 199 W. 8th Ave., Suite 3, Eugene, OR 97401.

Resource Publications
An Imprint of Wipf and Stock Publishers
199 W. 8th Ave., Suite 3
Eugene, OR 97401

www.wipfandstock.com

PAPERBACK ISBN: 978-1-6667-1580-4
HARDCOVER ISBN: 978-1-6667-1581-1
EBOOK ISBN: 978-1-6667-1582-8

NOVEMBER 11, 2021

"God, I give you glory, and as I give you glory, please take your glory, because I want to see your glory."

I dedicate this book to my grandmothers,
Bishop Helen Odessa Gillis and Elder Thelma Lee Ruffin,
who are women I strive to be.

Contents

Acknowledgments | viii

List of Abbreviations | ix

Prologue: What's in a Name? | x
- *Chapter 1*　ELOHIM | 1
- *Chapter 2*　EL | 17
- *Chapter 3*　YHVH or YAHWEH | 40
- *Chapter 4*　God, The Father | 53
- *Chapter 5*　God, The Son | 75
- *Chapter 6*　Jesus Christ: The Chosen One | 83
- *Chapter 7*　Jesus Christ, The Savior | 94
- *Chapter 8*　The Revelation Names of Jesus Christ | 115
- *Chapter 9*　The Holy Spirit | 127

Epilogue | 145

Bibliography | 147

Acknowledgments

Ironically, I can hear the song lyrics, "if it had not been for the Lord on my side, where would I be?" Probably, in a ditch somewhere instead of struggling to write these acknowledgments. So, of course, I must thank God for all of his many benefits, including his grace and his mercy. Without his continued guidance, I would honestly be like a ship without a sail. For some reason, I hear many old devotional songs right now, which is kind of eerie, but I progress.

I am grateful for my family, especially for my two grandmothers who died before finishing this book. I picture Grandma Thelma holding the book, saying, "Ruffin, Ruffin, Ruffin," while Grammis saying to her best friend, "you really loved that old man, uh?" then slowly reading the title aloud and questioning, "you wrote this?" I miss you, two old ladies. Thank you so much for loving me.

I also want to acknowledge my mother and father, who have always supported me throughout my life. It was probably hard because I am such a private individual. Unlike Sheila, who reveals every idea, I keep everything under wraps. However, whenever an achievement comes to fruition, you are always equally proud. Thank you, Sheila, for keeping me on my toes as you are a go-getter; I am more laid back in my pursuit, probably because I'm older and tired. Either way, I am genuinely grateful. Thank you so much for loving me.

Lastly, I recognize the love of my life: my favorite child, Sammie. Hilarious, Arian. I love you so much. When I want to stop and rest on my laurels, I am reminded that I have to keep moving to keep achieving. I am so proud of your accomplishments, and I know that your father would be so proud of the young lady you are becoming. Always remember that I love you and that you can achieve great things. Thank you for letting me love you.

List of Abbreviations

ESV – English Standard Version
GNT – Good News Translations
KJV – King James Version
NIV – New International Version

Prologue

What's in a Name?

"WHAT'S IN A NAME? *That which we call a rose by any other name would it smell as sweet.*"[1] The first time I heard this infamous line was during a read-aloud in my sophomore English class. Juliet made a lot of sense. Sure, she was a starry-eyed teenager who was on the brink of suicidal demise, but her words still had meaning. After all, as children, we learned "sticks and stones may break our bones, but words will never hurt us." This phrase was echoed after being called a booger, snot rag, butt muncher, or even an African booty scratcher. Teachers taught this line in an all-out effort to help us ignore childhood banter and name-calling. However, if this was the case, then why did we frantically attempt to stop the insults before someone thought we did pick our noses, munched on butt, or was from Africa and, indeed, scratched booty?

Probably because our names can define who we are. After all, there is nothing wrong with being from Africa. However, it is an insult to be a booty scratcher, especially if it's not your own. No one wants to be called something they are not. Therefore, we attempt to stop the contemptuous name before it sticks. Being called a worthless sack continuously may result in a self-fulfilling prophecy, and the same can be said if somebody frequently called you "Beautiful" or "Gorgeous." Hear it enough, and you'll quickly forget that you look like the spawn of Jabba the Hut and Quasimodo.

Like Juliet, John Proctor was another character in a play entitled *The Crucible*, which dramatized Massachusetts's 1692 Salem witch trials. He was accused of witchery, set to hang, but could restore his life in exchange for a false confession. The offer seemed like a fair trade, his life for a lie. Nevertheless, his confession came with the price of nailing his name to the

---

1. Shakespeare, *Romeo and Juliet* 2.2, 46.

PROLOGUE

church door, condemning him of witchcraft. After learning this, Proctor changes his mind choosing death over a lie. All are puzzled why he would rather die instead of signing the declaration of guilt. Proctor boldly proclaimed, *"Because it is my name! Because I cannot have another in my life! Because I am not worth the dust on the feet of them that hang! How may I live without my name? I have given you my soul; leave me my name!"*[2]

Both play characters had different feelings when it came to their name, yet both faced fatality because of them. So, what's in a name? What's in a name that one person would be willing to reject their identity, but another would die for it. Can names be just mere labels that differentiate us from one another, or do they define who we are in this world? Are our names so invaluable that we can renounce them with ease, or are they worthy of death? The real question remains, what's in our name?

Analyzing the two fictional characters Juliet and John Proctor, we can see many of their characteristics within their names. Juliet's name is of Latin origin, meaning young or youthful. Juliet is a young, innocent maiden with a dignified predestined life in this Shakespearean tragedy. It is easy to see how her name demonstrates this youthfulness despite her growing in maturity throughout the play. Her name not only represented her age but her personality as she quickly falls in love with Romeo defying her family's wishes. Her youthful character is her downfall as she is met with a fatal fate and acts recklessly, taking her own life.

John is a Hebrew name that means "Jehovah has been gracious"[3] and has shown favor, demonstrates the Crucible character. Throughout the play, John struggles with a past act of infidelity, which he questions if God and his saintly wife, Elizabeth, can forgive him. Coincidentally, John also wrestles with forgiving himself despite his current honorable life. At the witch trial, John is unwilling to admit to adultery until he is met with an incredible offer: tell the truth and save his and his wife's life. Corrupting his good name, John tells the truth but tragically finds out that his wife lied to keep his integrity. John's willingness to forsake his honorable name ultimately demonstrated his goodness but sealed his fate.

It is unknown whether Shakespeare or Miller researched their two heroes' names; however, their names provided an additional layer for their character's development. Imagine if Shakespeare's play was titled "Romeo and Jacqueline." Would the character traits of "Jacqueline" portray this

---

2. Miller, *The Crucible*, 142.

3 "John," lines 1.

Prologue

youthful character when this name means "may God protect"[4]? Subliminally, would her tragic suicide be received more as tragic than romantic? What if John Proctor's name was Ricky Proctor? Would the character Ricky act powerfully as his name suggests versus how Proctor is portrayed? It appears that our names are important as each name has meaning and has power over our lives.

As a teenager, I loved flipping through my baby book. Usually, I would read about my past birthdays, touch the locks of my hair, or look at my adorable baby pictures as my mother wailed, *"what happened to you"* in the background. However, one day I came upon a page with the name "Spinvera Tytanisha." Questioning my mother about this peculiar name, I learned that it was for me. This was the name that my mother wanted to give her firstborn. After much laughter at her expense, we pondered how different my life would have been with such a "creative" name.

There was little to nothing about the origins or meanings of both of these names. To my knowledge, there was no digital fingerprint for anyone named Spinvera. Perhaps the name doesn't exist, that I would have been the first. Google search, however, found the name Tytanisha which was accompanied by court orders, charges, and arrest for several women with this name. Life for me probably would have been significantly different than having a name that means "God is gracious."[5] Gratefully, my mother had a change of heart from Spinvera Tytanisha to Shavonne Renee, with Renee meaning "reborn or born again,"[6] ultimately reshaping the course of my life.

When God made the covenant between Abram and Sarai, he changed their names to fit their new identity as. Abram's name meant "exalted father." Even though he was not a father, he was a surrogate one to his nephew Lot. However, once God promised him that his descendants would outnumber the stars, he changed his name to Abraham, meaning "father of many nations." God could have easily kept Abram's first name, but it did not shape his new purpose.

Consequently, Sarai's name meant " contentious and quarrelsome,"[7] which fit her nagging persistence in attempting to rush God's promise and her relationship with Hagar. Nevertheless, God changed her name to Sarah, which has several meanings: the most profound being "princess of

---

4. Ratnam, "60 Saint Names," line 50.
5. "Shavonne," line 2.
6. "Renee," line 2.
7. "Sarai," line 3.

the multitudes." Her new name indicated God taking ownership of her life as "the mother of all nations"[8] versus her previous controversial behaviors. The altering of these two names shows forth how their futures changed by merely changing a few letters.

Isaac and Rebekah named their son Jacob, which seemed to shape his entire life until he wrestled with God (Gen. 32:22–28). Before this event, Jacob lived up to his name as it means "supplant, undermines, or grabs,"[9] as he held on to his brother Esau's heel when they were being born. Even as the two grew older, Jacob coveted his brother's blessings as the firstborn. He tricked his father, grabbing hold of the birthright. After fleeing for many years, God told Jacob to return to his country. Sending his family before him, Jacob was left alone to wrestle with God. It appears that Jacob was living up to his name again as he grabbed on to God and wouldn't let go until he blessed him. Due to this encounter, God changed Jacob's name to Israel because he struggled with him and prevailed, ultimately concluding the covenant between Abraham and God becoming the father of the twelve tribes.

Simon was a fisherman whose name means "to listen,"[10] and undoubtedly, he heard the voice of God beckoning him to become a fisherman of men. As Simon followed Jesus, he listened to his teachings with his ears and heart as he was the first to respond to his question concerning who he was. Simon boldly proclaimed that Jesus was the Messiah, the Son of God, which changed the course of his life. Jesus honored him by changing his name to Cephas or Peter, which means "stone,"[11]; making Peter the rock he would build his church. Peter went from someone who listened to someone who would be heard as he was a bold advocate for our Lord and Savior Jesus Christ. The name changes of these individuals support that names can shape a person's destiny.

This is why much emphasis is placed on the perfect baby name. Parents obsess over this choice attempting to choose that particular name to give their offspring. Whether it's cultural, unique, biblical, or practical, there is a story behind every name. No parent throws a moniker on their precious baby boy or girl without explanation. Names have a purpose as it is one of

---

8. "Sarah", lines 96–98.
9. "Jacob," line 3.
10. "Simon," line 2.
11. "Peter", lines 1–3.

Prologue

our most prized commodities. Without one, we would have no identity as our destination would be as empty as someone calling us, "hey you."

No one likes their names to be misspelled or mispronounced as it is their unique character within this world. This is why much importance is placed on names within the Bible. God tells us that a good name is better than great riches or precious ointments (Prov. 22:1; Eccl. 7:1). It is practical to suggest that most people would like to be rich evidence of the Mega Millions craze. However, these verses implore us to value our names over being wealthy, which reasonably suggests that our names have greater worth than riches. Our names are a representation of our character as we live with them every single day. We tend to want to protect them in the simplest form of spelling and articulation, yet we must guard our name by having a good reputation.

A Scottish proverb says, "a bad wound may heal, but a bad name will kill." This proverb corresponds to Proverbs 10:7, which states, "the memory of the righteous is blessed, But the name of the wicked will rot." These epigrams suggest that there is life in a good name, but on the other hand, there is death. Ironically, most people do not die because of their names, but a bad reputation can destroy our status. There are times when we are guilty of an offense but are willing to lie to protect our good name. If this were not the case, then Peter would have readily confessed to knowing Jesus versus denying him (Luke 22:54–62), choosing to safeguard his reputation.

Our names are important as they represent us. Often people share names, but our personalities are different. For example, archaeologists believed that there were over seventy tombs with the name Yeshua (Jesus) before Jesus' death. This name also was mentioned within the old testament (II Chr. 31:15; Ezra 2:2). Even though it does not provide great detail concerning these individuals, it supports that this name was used before the birth of Jesus Christ. Another form of this name, Yehoshua, was also used before our Lord and Savior's name. As time passed, the name transformed from Greek to Hebrew, and the spelling became "*Iesus*" and then later Jesus. Ironically, many people had this name before God's beloved Son, which means "God rescues."[12] Perhaps these individuals' destinies were shaped by their names. However, we do know that the name Jesus Christ is the embodiment of salvation for the world.

God has established this one name above every name, and in the end, every knee will bow, and every tongue shall confess that he is Lord

---

12. "What does the name Jesus mean," lines 14–15.

(Phil. 2:9–11). However, many of us can make this confession now before He comes, while others can't because they do not know him. Possibly, the reason why many people do not know God is that they do not know his name. When we are introduced to others, we exchange our names, giving subliminally, if not consciously, the definition of our identity. Therefore, how can we honestly say we know God if we limit him to one name?

Our God is beyond a one-name moniker. This book will explore the meaning behind God's name, Jesus Christ, and the Holy Spirit. Since God is three persons in one, it is befitting to examine each of the Godhead's names. It is vital to understand who God is and what he says He is to his people in our Christian walk. At the central part of our understanding, we must acknowledge him in all our ways, and the first step is determining what we call him. Some may call him Savior; however, how can someone identify him in this role if they believe He has not saved them from anything. How can a person call him a healer if they genuinely have never been sick? The book's purpose is to help close the gap on some of God's mysteries through his many names. As we examine and learn about the names of God, the Father, God the Son, and God, the Holy Spirit, we will truthfully answer the question, "what's in a name"?

Chapter 1

ELOHIM

In the beginning, God created the heaven and the Earth.

GENESIS 1:1

TO FULLY COMPREHEND THE names of God, we must start at the beginning. God's mighty power was unfolded in the book of Genesis, establishing that He is the creator of everything. It is incredible to think that God created the Earth and all that inhabits it through his divine wisdom. Therefore, without God, there was nothing, but with him came everything. When his spirit moved upon the water, He was able to give form to the world. With just a few words from God, the light came into existence, and with a few breaths, man became a living being. These miraculous acts define the first name of God, *Elohim*, which means the supreme and mighty one.[1]

Our natural minds cannot comprehend God's true divine omnipotence. Imagine if we were given the task to create a new universe without knowledge of the current world. It would be impossible for us to construct without some type of blueprint. Therefore, many scientists are challenged by the creation and evolution of man. Debates concerning the creation of the universe are continuously ongoing. It isn't easy to comprehend the world's formation when there are over one billion galaxies and trillions of stars. Jupiter, the largest planet, is three hundred times larger than Earth,

---

1. Leake, "What does Elohim mean", line 12.

and OGLE-2016-BLG-1190Lb, a newfound planet is roughly thirteen times larger than Jupiter.[2] Eighteen billion dollars is spent in the National Aeronautics and Space Administration (NASA) annually searching for these mysterious answers.[3] However, the simple reality is that the God of strength and power created the universe in a matter of six days.

In the beginning, *Ruach Elohim*[4], which is the Spirit of God, rested on the empty void, and the Earth was formed (Gen 1:2). The term ruach in Hebrew means spirit, wind, or breath. This name is referenced as the Spirit of God, which is a life-giving source. The spirit moved over the water to create the land formations causing the world to become alive. The spirit also gave life to Adam, fashioning him into a living soul (Gen 2:7). Ironically, this is the same breath that occupies our lungs today. God freely gave his ruach to the just as well as the unjust for us to have life. The difference is that our lives are more abundant because the Spirit of God not only dwells within our lungs but wholly lives inside of us.

On several occasions within the Bible, the Spirit of God has been described as wind (Ezek 37:9–14, Acts 2:2). The wind moves air, and despite a full understanding of where it comes from or where it goes, we tend to know that it is there. So, it is with the Spirit of God (John 3:8). God's ruach moves unpredictably, which can be like forceful hurricane winds colliding with our flesh to remove unneeded debris from our lives, or it can be as gentle as a summer's breeze refreshing us from the heat of the day. "Wind is called a renewable energy source because the wind will blow as long as the sun shines." The ruach of God is an energy source that regenerates us daily. As long as the Son of God shines, so will the Ruach of God continue to blow.

Elohim is the plural of the root word El, which means god, concluding that God is deemed three Gods in One: God the Father, God the Son, and God the Holy Spirit.[5] Despite Christians not wanting to recognize this, there are also other gods within the universe. God, himself, orders us in the commandments stating, "Thou shalt have no other gods before me" (Exod 20:3), implying that there are indeed other perceived supernatural beings, which are man-created. In polytheism, different cultural mythologies believe in more than one god. Some of the most known gods are Egyptian,

---

2. "Discovery", lines 2-3.
3. "Is NASA's budget", lines 4149.
4. "What does the Hebrew word "ruach mean," lines 1–8.
5. "Why is Elohim plural," lines 1– 2.

Greek, Hindu, and Norse pantheon. These cultures put their faith in gods named Ra (Egyptian), Zeus (Greek), Brahma (Hindu), and Odin (Norse), and even with their so-called powers, they still have several deities in each religion[6]. Despite, there being many false gods, God is *Elohay Elohim*, God of gods.[7]

For this very cause, God warns his people to serve him, the true and living God, *Elohim Chaiyim*.[8] Recognizably, different gods are counterfeit, attempting to resemble the true God of Israel. However, God proves that He alone is the true and living God as he kept his promises concerning those who worshipped pagan gods. Elohim Chaiyim stated that He would destroy them, cast them out of the land, and punish them with death (Deut 17:2–7, Exod 22:20, and Exod 23:33). Therefore, Joshua's last message to the Israelites in Shechem was so profound as he knew the fate that awaited those who did not recognize God as God of gods. In chapter 24, Joshua's prophetic words reminded the Israelites of God's strength and power, which was used to deliver them on numerous occasions. Joshua admonished the people to serve the Lord in spirit and truth lest they fall into dire situations.

Before the Israelites became a great nation, several of their forefathers had worshipped pagan gods. Undoubtedly, this was true for Terah, Abraham's father. Joshua calls Terah out in verse two by saying. "Long ago your ancestors, including Terah the father of Abraham and Nahor, lived beyond the Euphrates River and worshipped other gods." In reviewing the genealogy of Terah, it appears that he was a descendant of Noah's son Shem. This verse is impressive because Abraham's father knew Noah personally for over a hundred years after the flood. Realistically, Noah had to mention God's mighty power concerning "the flood," yet Abraham's father continued to serve pagan gods. Astonishingly, it appears impossible to think that anyone would serve other gods after hearing Noah's story. Yet, the reality is that we still have many Terah spirits in our churches today who witness God's sovereign power but still refuse to believe.

Noah's miracle and Terah's response is almost a foreshadowing of what is happening in our world today. As Christian believers, we have read biblical accounts of God's strength and power on numerous occasions. We can recount the miraculous works He did throughout the old and new testament. However, those events occurred thousands of years ago, and as

---

6. Gill, "List of Gods" lines 9–43.
7. "Elohay Elohim", line 3.
8. "Elohim Chaiyim", line 3.

human beings, we desire tangibility. For some of us, if we do not see it, we cannot believe it. Indicating why Terah continued to serve pagan gods, even after Noah's encounter.

There are people in our world, even Christians, who deny the full power and authority of God because of spiritual disabilities such as weak faith, spiritual blindness, deafness to God's word, cognitive impairments, and spiritual retardation. We witness God's power but are handicapped by our understanding. Waters continue to flood the Earth just as people are still being raised from the dead. However, due to our spiritual disabilities, we rely on meteorologists and physicians instead of God's power. It is God alone who can produce earthquakes, tsunamis, tornados, and volcanic eruptions. Just as God's wisdom is given to man to cure diseases. We can try to comprehend these so-called natural events as scientific propaganda, yet real understanding cannot happen unless it comes from God.

Since God is not limited to being sovereign over one aspect of life, it is suitable for his name to be mentioned in the plural sense. Throughout the Hebrew Bible, Elohim or Elohay is combined with other words to describe God's many characteristics.[9] Being that God has authority over all, he must have names that classify his power within the heavens and the Earth. We, as his creation, have a few names that distinguish our identity; therefore, it would be suitable that the Almighty God have several names that define his massive characteristics.

Moses declared God as *Elohay Kedem*, the God of the Beginning (Deut 33:27). The first phrase of the Bible states, "In the beginning, God created the heaven and the earth" (Gen 1:1). There was nothing before our God until he spoke it into existence. Life begins with him as well as death. Nothing can start within our lives unless the almighty God wills it. He is "Alpha and Omega, the beginning and the end, the first and the last" (Rev 22:12). Every blessing begins with God as well as every curse. Thus, we must ensure that we pursue God's righteousness to obtain life and blessings instead of curses and death. As believers, if we keep God as our launching point, we can rise to greatness.

Imagine how much more meaningful life would be if we started our life, even our day off with God. Joyce Meyers once said, "The key to having God's abundant life is keeping him in his rightful place in our priorities."[10] God's rightful place is being first in our lives in every aspect of our day.

---

9. "Names of God", lines 10–19.
10. Meyers, "Putting God First," lines 28–29.

ELOHIM

Surrendering our will to him will allow our God to direct us on the right path (Prov 3:5–6). Fundamentally, God's will is perfect and just; and if we allow him to take the lead, He will guide us with the compass of his divine power and strength.

Unfortunately, this was not the case for the Israelites when they were faced with the Assyrian army. They did not keep God at the forefront of their plans. Instead of seeking God's will, they resorted to forming alliances with Egypt. Being motivated by fear and doubt, the Israelites sought answers to problems that only God could solve. However, God warned Judah and stated, He was *Elohay Mishpat,* God of Justice (Isa 30:18). It is God's good pleasure to fight for his children; however, when we attempt to fight our own battles, we tend to rely on those who are weaker than God.

Our God is a God of justice as it is written in Romans 12:19, "Dearly beloved, avenge not yourselves, but rather give place unto wrath: for it is written, Vengeance is mine; I will repay, saith the Lord." Retaliation is an unbeliever's best weapon and a Christian's worst enemy. Our world is filled with people seeking revenge for wrongdoings. Our televisions are filled with lawsuit commercials, reality-based court shows, and judges bring down the hammer of justice. Sometimes, suing can lead to big payouts, but what does it cost in the end. God is the best judge because he has all the evidence. Nothing gets by him. Therefore, as Christians, we do not have to "get mad or get even," yet we can count it all joy knowing that Elohay Mishpat will handle every case.

In Micah, chapter 6, God himself holds a mock trial to determine what faults his chosen people had against him. God called on the mountains to be his witnesses. Ironically, these were the same mountains that witnessed altars built for the pagan gods. God chose these same high places to show that he is *Elohay Marom,* God of Heights[11]. Within this chapter, God reminded the Israelites of the miracles He performed for them, and yet they continued to provide meaningless sacrifices religiously. Micah 6:6–7 includes a list of the sacrifices the people were giving to God despite remaining in sin. Ironically, these were the same empty promises they offered the false gods. God is the high God, who did not want insincere offerings, yet he wanted the people to be righteous and be humble before him.

God does not delight in pointless sacrifices or promises (Isa 1:11–15). To atone for their sins, the Israelites would give God burnt offerings, feast, and blood offerings of goats, bullocks, and lambs. However, God saw the

---

11. "Names of God," line 14.

hollowness of these sacrifices. They were pointless and meaningless unto God. God was not convinced that the people repented for their sins as they acted religiously, but not spiritually. Dutifully, the people would bring these sacrifices to God because it was the right thing to do. God had commanded them to provide these offerings. Even though the Israelites were obedient to the act, they were not obedient to God's will. The sacrifices were meant to show true repentance; however, if there was no true offering for forgiveness, how could the Israelites call it a sacrifice.

Sacrifice means "an act of giving up something valued for the sake of something else regarded as more important or worthy."[12] Sin has the highest cost; the cost of our lives (Rom 6:23). Indeed, God did require the burnt offerings and festivals as this was the Mosaic Law. However, those sacrifices were invaluable if the meaning of the offering was lost. The Israelites sin was more significant than the empty offerings that they delivered unto God. God only saw the blood on their hands instead of what the blood should have represented.

Even in our churches today, we act religiously versus acting spiritually. We faithfully come to church on Sunday morning. We religiously take communion. We religiously pay our tithes, and we conscientiously sing songs of praise to God. However, are these empty offerings or tokens that we give God versus heartfelt sacrifices. God tells us to assemble ourselves and fellowship one with another (Heb 10:25) just as he told the Israelites how to establish the burnt offerings (Lev1:7). God requires all these things from us. However, if we are doing it without expectation from God or adoration for him, it is as empty as the Israelites' burnt offering.

God is a high god who delights in our sacrifices and our gratitude towards him. This is why he gave the ultimate sacrifice of his son, Jesus Christ. God knew that giving up his beloved son, that he valued, would produce something of greater worth and importance. Luke 15:7 states, "I say unto you, that likewise, joy shall be in heaven over one sinner that repenteth, more than ninety and nine just persons, which need no repentance." Jesus needed no repentance, for He was without sin. Nevertheless, God sacrificed his Son for an unjust people because He saw the value in us.

What an incredible thought, that the Almighty could find us worthy, to be even called children of God (I John 3:1). Taking inventory of our lives, we can see our successes, but often we are blinded by our failures. Disappointments in life can overtake us so much that we do not fulfill our

---

12. "Sacrifice", lines 20-21.

full purpose in God. Outwardly, we present a holy vessel through our appearance and countenance, yet internally we are guilt-driven by our past sins. We can only see our iniquities, despite God's saving grace. Regardless of our past transgressions, God sees who we are in him.

Numerous times, the Israelites fell short of God's glory, but within the context of Isaiah chapter 43, God tells them how extraordinary they are to him. In verse four, God said, "Since you are precious and honored in my sight, and because I love you, I will give people in exchange for you, nations in exchange for your life (NIV)." When the Israelites were released from Babylonian captivity, they were scattered by their adversary. However, God promised to reunite them. Even though this was written to Israel, it is still a declaration to believers called by God's name. Just as God rescued Israel, He saved us from our sins. He exchanged his Son, Jesus Christ, for our lives, and we will all be reunited when He comes.

The death of Jesus is the pathway to reconciliation with God. Sin separates us from him, and since the days of the Creation, God longs to have a relationship with us, as He did with Adam. Adam was the first human being ever to encounter God. Adam was not subjected to many of the elements that shape our adulthood. His nature was of God, and his nurture came from God. Unlike many of us who struggle to hear God's voice, Adam knew it well. His voice was the only one he heard before Eve being created. As believers, we will never have the relationship that Adam had with God while on Earth, as sin separates us from him. However, through the blood of Jesus Christ, we can be reunified with God through the power of his forgiveness.

Our God is *Elohay Selichot*. God of Forgiveness.[13] Nehemiah gave God this name when he was called to rebuild the walls of Jerusalem. Nehemiah had summoned God's people to repentance as not only were the walls of Jerusalem broken, but he found broken lives. Through Ezra, God renewed his covenant with his people. Nehemiah knew the people had to repent for him to do the impossible task of rebuilding Jerusalem's walls. God's forgiving power abundantly pardoned their sins. Not only this, but even under much oppression, God allowed the Israelites to rebuild Jerusalem's walls in fifty-two days. When God forgives us, it should bring confidence to do his will and use us in miraculous ways.

Besides Jesus, there was no one else who prepared the way more to Christianity than Apostle Paul. Before him, the gospel of Jesus Christ was only being taught to the Jews. However, through his ministry, the gospel

---

13. "Elohay Selichot", line 3.

spread throughout Asia, Greece, and the entire Roman Empire, even to the Gentiles. Paul's theology expanded beyond Jewish rituals and provided a foundation for believers to understand that Jesus Christ's death and resurrection were the means to salvation. Despite Paul's previous persecution of Christian believers, God pardoned him of his sins, saying, "This man is my chosen instrument to proclaim my name to the Gentiles and their kings and the people of Israel" (Acts 9:15 NIV). Through God's forgiving power, Paul's entire life changed from persecutor to persecuted for the sake of Jesus Christ.

As followers of Christ, we must learn how to do the simple act of forgiveness. Even though God commands it, it is one of the most challenging tasks to complete as Christians. Our brains are hardwired to remember the pain, whether it is physical or emotional. Most people can relate to being burned. When we approach the heating source, we naturally use caution to prevent from being scorched again. Ironically, this also happens when others emotionally burn us. Caution turns into avoidance, which then evolves into hate, which later can progress into sin.

It's easy to say we must forgive; however, on the contrary, it is more challenging to do it. Mahatma Gandhi once said, "The weak can never forgive. Forgiveness is the attribute of the strong".[14] Imagine the torment Jesus went through on Calvary, and at the face of death, he asked the Father to "forgive them, for they know not what they do" (Luke 23:34). This was the first of the seven sayings of Jesus while on the cross. Undergoing torment and agonizing death, he still asked God to forgive his persecutors. At this point, Jesus denied his needs for the sake of the entire world. This act of mercy and compassion is an example for us today as believers. Just as Jesus put aside his pain, He also tells us to follow suit. Jesus tells us to deny ourselves and follow him (Matt 16:24). This framework means that regardless of our pain, we must forgive others to pursue him.

Ironically, when we do not forgive, we ultimately tell God not to forgive us. Matthew 6:15, states, "But if you do not forgive others their sins, your Father will not forgive your sins (NIV)." Not forgiving others means we deny the meaning of the cross and the death of Jesus Christ. Jesus illustrated this parable in Matthew 18:23, concerning the forgiveness of debt among a particular servant. The king forgave the servant, but this same servant could not pardon his fellow man. Within the Lord's prayer, Jesus again talks about forgiveness stating, "forgive us our debts, as we also have

---

14. Gandhi, lines 1-3.

forgiven our debtors (Matt 6:12). There was no more outstanding debt than the cost that Jesus paid for our sins. The shedding of our Savior's blood blotted out our transgressions as the ultimate act of forgiveness. As Christians, when we struggle with forgiveness, we should think on Calvary at the willingness of Jesus to forgive our sins.

Jesus once again illustrated this readiness to forgive through the Prodigal Son parable. Within this parable, a man had two sons in which the youngest received his inheritance, spending it all on "riotous living." Frustrated, tired, and starving, the son returned to his father, seeking forgiveness. This parable is a demonstration of God's eagerness to forgive us of our sins. Imagine how the father must waited and watched daily for his son to return home to him. No doubt the father experienced emotional pain and suffering.

Ironically, God also experiences distress over the loss of his children. Just like the father waited for his son, God sits and waits for us. What was amazing about this parable was that the father saw his son even though he was "a long way off." Although it may seem we are distant from God, God is never too far away from us. He still sees us even if we seem detached from him. The good news is that we are not too far away from his forgiveness.

One of our divine rights as the sons and daughters of God is to have him nearby. Jeremiah called God *Elohay Mikarov*, which means a God who is near[15]. During this time, Israel was led by religious leaders seeking wisdom from false prophets instead of seeking counsel from God. In Jeremiah 23:23, God asked, "Am I a God at hand, saith the Lord, and not a God afar off? Therefore, Isaiah said we must seek the Lord while he is near (55:6–7). We must understand that God gives us ample time to seek his face while we live. Unfortunately, once we die, we will no longer have that right. While we still have the chance, we should take advantage of him being nearby.

Correspondingly, within the holy month of Elul, there is a saying, "The King is in the field." Most of the year, the kings would live enclosed by their palace doors, unreachable and unattainable to their subjects. Though, during the month of Elul, the king would actively walk among the people and hear their request. Using this parable shows how God, the great king, makes himself available to us despite our lowly state.[16] When God is near, we must seize the moment to receive from him "with a sincere heart in full

---

15. Names of God, line 15.
16. Richman, "The King", lines 15–19.

assurance of faith" (Heb 10:22). God being near allows us to touch him and permits him to touch our lives as well.

As Christian believers, we should purify our hearts and minds to become closer to God (Jas 4:8). Often, we are in God's presence, but we are absent from him. Indeed, this sounds like an oxymoron as there seemingly is no way to be present and absent simultaneously. Yet, this is a frequent occurrence within the body of Christ. After Jacob betrayed Esau, he had to flee for his life. No doubt, Jacob was plagued by his circumstances: traveling four hundred miles to Haran, leaving his home, as well as deceiving his father. However, God reassured him that He was still with him despite his situation. Due to this, Jacob proclaimed, "Surely the Lord is in this place; I knew it not" (Gen 28:16). Just like Jacob, we are often overwhelmed by our condition, which causes us to miss God.

Asaph, the psalmist, also confessed missing God's presence as he thought about the wicked's prosperity (Ps 73). He admits that he almost turned away from him due to the plight the righteous found themselves in compared to the ungodly. Without question, mostly every Christian has had these same thoughts. Our congregations are not filled with millionaires and, most times, are occupied with the financially weak. Poverty would cause anyone to ponder their relationship with God. Nevertheless, Asaph knew that his strength came from God, and those who were "far from him would perish" (verse 27). Like Asaph, we need to realize that it is better to be close to God and live versus being wealthy and eternally die.

Despite our circumstances, we must understand that being near to God is where we find our strength and refuge. Undeniably, this is why God is called *Elohay Mauzi,* God of my strength[17]. Even as Asaph thought about the wicked's success, he also understood that God is the strength of his heart (verse 26). No matter how physically and emotionally weak we become, we must stand firm in our belief that God will make us strong. During hardship, Paul said, "therefore I take pleasure in infirmities, in reproaches, in necessities, in persecutions, in distresses for Christ's sake; for when I am weak, then am I strong" (2 Cor 12:10). Our weakness allows God to manifest his divine strength within us.

It would be foolish for us to deny that our help and strength do not come from God. If we think about it, we were made from the dust of the Earth: weak, feeble, and without life. The only way that Adam became a living soul was by the breath of the almighty God. Therefore, as his children,

---

17. "Names of God," lines 14–15.

we should never be dismayed by our physical failings as God gives strength to those who are weary and increases the power of the weak (Isa 40:29). Accordingly, we can rest in the strength of our God as he tells us to "fear not, for I am with thee: be not dismayed; for I am thy God: I will strengthen thee; yea, I will help thee; yea, I will uphold thee with the right hand of my righteousness" (Isa 41:10).

As King David's life was coming to an end, he begins to think of God's delivering strength and salvation. David was a great king who fought great battles and had more remarkable victories (2 Sam 8). He could have attributed these victories to his skills as a warrior. However, he knew he could not win without the almighty help of God. God was his strength and his rock (Ps 18:1–2). David's comparison to God being his rock indicates the strength and solid foundation he found in the Father. In the natural sense, it takes a powerful force to break a rock. However, within the spirit, we can stand on the rock of our salvation that can never be broken.

David made this declaration that God is *Elohay Yishi*[18]. God of my salvation. In Psalm 62:2. David confirms that God is his rock and his salvation, his fortress, and he will not be greatly shaken (ESV). This is a bold affirmation that God is not only his solid foundation but also a fortress when he needs to be saved. A fortress is a "heavily protected and impenetrable building," which appears to describe the salvation of our God. As believers, we have excellent protection from the wicked when we call on the name of the Lord. His name alone is a strong tower where the righteous can run and be saved (Prov 18:10).

Within this psalm (62), David also refers to God as being the horn of his salvation (verse 2). Just as animals use their horns as a defense mechanism against predators, God also protects us against our adversary. Animals also use their horns to establish their territory, among other prey. This ritual is to show dominance and to protect other vulnerable animals within the herd. God's domain is "the earth and the fulness thereof" (Ps 24:1). Therefore, indicating that no evil can overtake God's children as long as He has dominion power in the Earth. He is a horn of salvation ready to shield us from the enemies' predatorial devices.

Psalms often mentioned the saving grace of God. The gift of salvation is granted through Jesus Christ. God freely gives salvation and the gift of eternal life through him; however, many have rejected this gift of redemption. It's likened to a child receiving stocks for Christmas versus the latest

---

18. "Names of God," lines 17–18.

gaming system. Despite the stocks having more significant value, the child instantly runs to the new game because it's tangible and exciting. They cannot see the stocks' worth because of their long-term impact as the XBOX brings instant gratification. This is how the world is when it comes to the gift of salvation. Many run after the lust of the world because it brings immediate fulfillment versus having eternal life.

There are times we receive gifts, and to our bewilderment, we are unable to recognize what it is. This is often the issue with unbelievers and those who do not recognize the cross's perfect gift. Likewise, it is also the church's issue, as we often discuss how to become saved but infrequently discuss the real benefits of this lasting gift. Being saved from sin frees us from being enslaved to sin. Slavery brings forth imprisonment, mistreatment, and unconditional submission. When we are enslaved to sin, we are captive and victimized by our adversary. It feels like chains bind us, and some have said to be in a zombie state of submission. However, the gift of God brings forth many benefits of salvation. As Christians, we understand the notion of being freed by the blood of Jesus and being a child of God. However, unbelievers may not be able to comprehend what is not palpable.

Countless times we have heard testimonies about God's salvation, and each time the experience is different for everyone. There comes a time in every sinners' life when they become emotionally tired. Exhaustion from ongoing sin simply overtakes them. However, in their weariness comes a moment of clarity in which they realize "enough is enough." For those who reach this confession comes salvation. It is suitable for unbelievers to understand the spiritual benefits of salvation. However, it is equally essential for them to recognize that God will save them even from themselves.

As Christians, we proudly proclaim that we are saved from our sins. However, the actual question is, what are we saved from? This question should not produce a cookie-cutter response as salvation is an individual process. God keeps us from whatever sin we were committing. He doesn't have to save a liar from prostitution or a thief from alcoholism, yet God meets the need for salvation wherever redemption is required. God promises in his word that if we believe in our hearts and confess with our mouth that Jesus Christ is Lord and rose from the dead that He will save us from ourselves (Rom 10:9).

God's commitment is being a Holy God, *Elohim Kedoshim*[19]. To save us from our sins, God admonishes his people to be holy because He is holy

---

19 "Names of God", line 19.

ELOHIM

(Lev 19:2). Often as Christians, we utilize the word holy to describe God. However, we often do not understand the meaning. God being holy means that he consecrates himself to us and sets himself apart for our good. Therefore, he wants us to be set apart for him. Even though God is an omnipotent God, he has set rules that govern his sovereign power to benefit those who believe in him.

One of those rules is that God cannot lie. God is all-powerful. If he chose to lie, then who could stop him? Yet, this is a rule God set for us because God is holy. He cannot go back on his Word. Therefore this requires us, as God's children, to stand firm on every promise.

God also has a rule that if we repent, He is faithful and just, forgiving us from all our sins (1 John 1:9). No matter how often we fall short of God's glory, he is ready and eagerly waiting to forgive us. Imagine an unfaithful spouse that commits adultery continuously. No doubt, we would draw the line of forgiveness because the act was committed obsessively. However, this is what happens with God. We, as the brides of Christ, commit spiritual adultery against him when we delight in worldly pleasures (Jas4:4). Jesus commanded us to forgive continuously, seventy times seven (Matt 18:22), because his Father unceasingly forgives us.

Look at God's dedication to his people. The entire Bible is filled with promises from God. If we are weary, he will give us strength (Isa 40:29). If we are afraid, God said he would be with us (Deut 31:8). If we are bound, He will set us free (John 8:36). If we give unto him what is right, God will open the floodgates of heaven (Mal 3:10). If we delight in the Lord, He will provide the desires of our heart (Ps 37:4). If we call on him, he will deliver us (Ps 50:15), and if we believe in him, he will give us eternal life (John 3:36). These are the promises that God offers because of his great dedication towards his children.

Another aspect of God being holy is the holiness of God. God is set apart from any other being in all the Earth. There is no one like him. In one encounter, Moses stated, "Who is like unto thee, O Lord, among the gods? who is like thee, glorious in holiness, fearful in praises, doing wonders?" (Exod 15:11). Moses witnessed God's holiness firsthand as He saw the plagues overtake the Egyptians. He understood that nothing or no one could match the splendor of God. In Revelation 4:8, it states that the angels proclaim God's holiness, day and night, never ceasing to say "holy, holy, holy, the Lord God, the Almighty, Who was and who is and who is to come." (Rev 4:8).

This declaration gives great joy to believers as God is *Elohay Tehilati*, God of my praise[20]. Within the Bible, no one praised God like King David. He had many reasons to bless God. After all, he was a mere shepherd boy when he was chosen to be King of Judah and Israel. God spared his life despite King Saul's several attempts to kill him (I Sam 18:11–27; 19:1–23; 23:25; 24:2, and 26:2), and he won several victories as a great warrior and a great king (I Chr 18). Within Psalms 18, David gives a detailed account of the achievements that God gave unto him. In the third verse, he proclaims, "I called to the Lord, who is worthy of praise, and I have been saved from my enemies."

It appears that praise was effortless for David as God blessed him throughout his life. Yet, one of the reasons why God called David "a man after his own heart" wasn't because David praised God during his successes, but he also blessed God during hardship. Psalms 13 was thought to be one of David's lowest points in his life. This psalm was written when David fled from Saul into the Cave of Adullam. While in the cave, David felt that God had forgotten him. He found himself in a terrible position as his beloved ally was trying to kill him, and he had to hide in the Philistine's camp, which was his sworn enemy.

When people are faced with two difficult situations, there's a saying "stuck between a rock and a hard place." Indeed, this could describe David's case. However, despite feelings of despair, he ended his prayer with "I will sing unto the LORD because he hath dealt bountifully with me" (verse 6). Even though it might have been easy for David to give up his faith, he knew that the hard place he finds himself was no match for the rock of his salvation. Despite the hard place, David chose the Rock.

Just as David did, we must praise God through life's difficult times. David stated, "I will lift up my eyes unto the hills, whence cometh my help. My help cometh from the Lord, which made heaven and earth" (Ps 121:1–2). David understood that the cave and the hills were a temporary help while he hid from Saul. However, David realized that his direct aid came from the Lord, worthy of his praise.

God admonishes the praises of his people. Praise is likened to a sport's team. When the crowd cheers, it appears that the team gets invigorated no matter how far they are trailing behind. When we praise God, He will perform miracles for us because we have ignited him.

---

20. "Names of God," line 15.

ELOHIM

There are several accounts of how praise kindled the Spirit of God to move on his people's behalf. When the Moabites and the Ammonites came against the people of Judah, King Jehoshaphat turned to God. Understanding that God would give them victory, the people instantly began to worship God, while others showed thunderous praise. As the people prepared themselves to face their enemies, Jehoshaphat prepared the singers and musicians to go first with praise. Before they got to the battle, Judah's people had already won, for all their enemies were dead. On the deceased were great riches, so much that it took three days to collect. Once again, the people assembled themselves in the valley of Berachah to bless God for his mighty acts. When they returned to Jerusalem, the people began to praise God again because the Lord had done miraculous works for them (2 Chr 20). The people praised God before, during, and after the battle. This is a lesson for believers that our praise should be continuous because we anticipate that God will give us the victory.

No matter what situations we find ourselves in, the key to victory is in our praise. After proclaiming the gospel of Jesus Christ, Paul and Silas were stripped, beaten, and thrown into jail. Despite their condition, they begin to sing songs of praise to God. Astonishingly, when they started to sing, an earthquake came and loosed them from their bondage (Acts 16:16-40). Praising God in hard times will loosen us from the overwhelming bondage that hardship brings. Despite the circumstances, we must understand there is power in our praise.

In reviewing the name Elohim, we have seen several accounts of God possessing many characteristics for his chosen people, such as forgiveness, strength, and praise. However, in the plural sense, Elohim may also refer to the Holy Trinity, one God in three persons. Christian belief states that there is only one eternal God; however, He exists within three people: God the Father, God the Son, and God the Holy Spirit. Often, they are referred to as the Godhead, three divine persons in one single God.

In Genesis 1:26-27, God says, "Let us make man in our image." There has been an ongoing debate concerning why God used the pronoun *us*. Some theologians believe that God may have been speaking in the plural sense because he was signifying his majesty in the Earth. However, it is further believed that God was speaking to God the Son and God the Holy Spirit. Meaning that Jesus and the Holy Spirit were there in the beginning. John 1:1 states, "In the beginning was the Word, and the Word was with God, and the Word was God." The Word was God the Son, who we know as Jesus. Also, in Genesis 1:2 it states that God's spirit moved upon the void, which implies that the Holy Spirit was also in the beginning. Concluding that when God said, "Let us make," he referred to the Godhead of the Son and the Spirit.

In Paul's farewell message to the church of Corinth, he states, "The grace of the Lord Jesus Christ, and the love of God, and the communion of the Holy Ghost, be with you all" (2 Cor 13:14). Paul reveres the Holy Trinity by giving the Godhead three distinctive characteristics, grace, love, and communion. The grace of Jesus Christ is the "free and unmerited favor God"; the love of God is the unwavering affection he gives to his people, and the communion of the Holy Spirit is the intimate relationship that connects us to the Father. The scriptural meaning clearly shows how the Trinity is joined in the form of one God, concluding that the name Elohim could have been used in the plural sense to describe one God is three persons.

The name of God, Elohim, classifies the true essence of God as it describes his limitless power and characteristics. He is one God in many forms. Throughout this chapter, we discovered God as the creator having dominion over all things. We also learned that there are several gods within the world, yet He is the true and living God. In examining God's name, we realized how his name is associated with many other traits that exemplify his glory in all the Earth. Lastly, we were able to conclude that God is one God in three persons: God the Father, God the Son, and God the Holy Spirit. God's name Elohim indeed indicates that our God is the God of Strength and Power.

Chapter 2

EL

And he blessed him, and said, blessed be Abram of the most high God, possessor of heaven and Earth.

GENESIS 14:19

EL IS THE ROOT word from Elohim, which refers to God's strength, power, and might[1]. This singular form of God's name shows his solitary rule and control overall. When unifying the church, Paul stated in Ephesians 4:6, "One God and Father of all, who is above all, and through all, and in you all." Paul was showing that we are of one body, one faith, and one God. For this very reason, "God can do exceedingly abundantly above all that we ask or think, according to the power that worketh in us (Ephesian 3:20)." These key verses show that God has absolute rule over all the Earth through his great power and might.

Often, God is revered as omnipotent, omniscient, and omnipresent. The origin of the word "Omni" stems from Latin, meaning all[2]. The word all means that something is complete or without limits; it encompasses everything. If we take the first part of Ephesians 4:6 and substitute the word "all" for the word "everything," it would read "One God and Father of *everything*, who is above *everything*." Scripturally it clearly displays God's supremacy

---

1. "The Meaning," lines 6–8.
2. "Omni", line 1.

over all that is in the world. God's power is not limited. He has rule over every disease, over every financial issue, over every emotion, every thought, and every relationship. He has no restrictions; however, our lack of faith puts constraints on him.

God is omnipotent; he has power over *everything*. This declaration means that God has full capacity, which is unhampered, unobstructed, and unhindered. In Jeremiah 32, God told Jeremiah to purchase land, which was currently occupied by the Babylonian army. This was a questionable purchase because Jeremiah was held prisoner by the very same army God told him to request the land. Despite his obedience, Jeremiah still had some doubts. God answered Jeremiah saying, "Behold, I am the Lord, the God of all flesh is anything too difficult for Me?" (Jer 32:27). That question still rings true today. Often in our Christian walk, we will have a Jeremiah moment, especially when faced with an impossible task. However, the omnipotent God is still saying, "Is there anything too difficult for Me?" We must pray that our answer will always be, "no, there is nothing too difficult for our God."

God is omniscient; He is the all–knowing God; He knows *everything*. For this cause, God is called the God of Knowledge, *'El De'OT*[3]. It should bring great comfort to know that God knows our beginning and our end. In Jeremiah 29:11, the Lord shares that He knows the plans that He has for us. Often, Christians believe that this Scripture means that we will not witness hardship. This cannot be further away from the truth. Peter explained that we would have trials and tribulations to try our faith (1 Pet 4:12). However, God always makes a battle plan for victory. Therefore, God knows every pain and every challenge we will face on Earth; however, He also knows our victories.

The Bible is filled with several characters who faced great adversity. Job lost his health, his children, and his wealth. However, Job still held on to his faith, saying, "Though he slay me, yet will I trust in him" (Job 13:15). At the hands of his brother, Joseph was sold into slavery, charged with rape, and placed in prison before becoming Egypt's ruler. John the Baptist had to set himself apart to announce the arrival of the Messiah. Despite his great zeal to fulfill his purpose, his uncompromising message was met with death. Apostle Paul is credited for spreading Christianity to the masses, yet he was thrown in prison on numerous occasions, stoned but lived, and later beheaded in Rome. God knows we will experience trials and tribulations

---

3. "Names of God," lines 22–23.

in our lives. However, we must live for Christ because, in our suffering, he will be glorified.

God is Omnipresent; He is *everywhere*. Indeed, there have been times we tried to hide from God, whether it was due to sin or because He had given us an incredible task. Adam and Eve were the first to play Hide and Seek with God due to their disobedience (Gen 3: 7–11). We can try to hide from God, but "ready or not," He will always find us. Like Adam and Eve, when we sin, we are naked before God, choosing not to have his protective covering. However, God is omnipresent, patiently waiting for us to give up the childish game and come out of hiding.

Getting an impossible task from God may cause us to become a runaway Christian, like Jonah who was given a great responsibility to speak against the city of Nineveh. God's request was startling. After all, Nineveh was an evil city that ruled by sheer terror. Their military tactics were greatly feared as the world knew them to massacre and torture their enemies. Of course, Jonah tried to run away from his charge. Like many of us, Jonah looked at his ability and leaned towards his understanding instead of depending on God. God's arms are long enough to reach us wherever we may be. When faced with our impossible task, just know that the omnipresent God is there.

God is All Powerful and All Knowing, there is no escape from him. David proclaimed, "Whither shall I go from thy spirit or whither shall I flee from the presence? If I ascend up into heaven, thou art there; if I make my bed in hell, behold, thou art there." (Ps 139:7). He knew that God dwells everywhere; even the darkness and the light are the same to God. God abides everywhere, and for this cause, God's name is attributed to specific places in heaven and on Earth.

In Genesis, God told Jacob to return to Bethel after his father-in-law, Laban, refused to give him what was rightfully his. Jacob built an altar there and named the place *El Bethel*, the House of God[4]. Jacob dedicated Bethel to God as God was his refuge, even when he fled from his brother Esau. Jacob also called God *El' Elohe Yisrael*, the God of Israel[5]. This proclamation was the personal relationship that God had with Jacob, who God named Israel. Indeed, God was with Jacob, even as Moses blessed his children, proclaiming that God is *El Yeshurun*, the God of Jeshurun, a poetic name for

---

4. "El Bethel," line 2.
5. "El' Eloe Yisrael," line 2.

Israel (Jacob)[6]. These different names represented places and showed God's dedication to Jacob, the Patriarch of the Israelites.

Elah Yisrael is another name meaning the God of Israel[7]. In this reference, Haggai and Zechariah proclaimed that God was the god over the nation of Israel. During the post-exilic time, the Jews returned to rebuild the temple in Jerusalem (Ezra 5:1). When the Persian governors inquired who permitted them to rebuild, the elders answered *Elah Sh'maya V'Arah*, the God of Heaven and Earth[8]. Eighty years after the first Jews returned from Babylonia, Ezra came with authority from King Artaxerxes, proclaiming that he would give the gold and silver to *Elah Yerush'lem*, God of Jerusalem[9], and *Elah Sh'maya*, God of Heaven[10]. How phenomenal was this declaration from the King of Persia, who practiced Zoroastrianism and worshipped other Persian gods? Ezra's book displays how God's sovereign power can destroy barriers and give unlikely support when we are in need.

Not only does God break barriers, but He proves himself as the true and living God, '*El Chay*[11]. There is no other god besides our Lord as they pale in comparison to our God because He is present (Isa 45:5). When we state that the Lord is true, we understand that he is genuine and authentic. Our God is alive because we can prove his existence.

Being a mere boy, David overcame a vicious warrior, and Daniel escaped the lions' snares. Imagine what would have happened if David attempted to use his strength, and Daniel called on the golden image to save him. Indeed, they would have been met with a different fate. However, with both occurrences, the Philistines and Nebuchadnezzar had to recognize that both young men served a living God.

Elijah was another person within the Bible who proved God's existence. In I Kings 18:20–24, it tells how Elijah and the prophets of Ba'al both made altars to their gods. This demonstration was to prove that one god was mightier than the other. The Ba'al worshippers cried unto their god to accept their altars by fire. Despite their wailing and even self-mutilation, nothing happened. Being confident in the Lord's presence, Elijah saturated the alters with water before calling on the true and living God. To the Ba'al

6. "Forty-four El Names," line 14.
7. "Hebrew Names," line 93.
8. Elah Sh'maya V'Arah," line 3.
9. "Hebrew Names," linr 94.
10. "Hebrew Names," line 95.
11. "Names of God", line 5.

worshippers' surprise, the almighty God did not only light the altar but consumed it along with the water within the trenches showing forth his existence in a powerful way.

Psalm 136 is also a testament to God's power, strength, and might. When King Jehoshaphat led his armies into victory, this was the song they sang. Throughout this psalm, the writer praised *'El Ha Shamayim*, The God of Heaven[12], "for his mercy endureth forever." This song of praise gave several instances in which God delivered the Israelites. The composer offers praise to God for the great works He created. He praises God for delivering the Israelites out of Egypt, parting the Red Sea, and allowing them to endure the wilderness. The praise continued as he recounts how God defeated great kings and their enemies to bring them to the land of their inheritance.

Our God is a great and mighty God, given the names' *El Haggadol* (the great god) and *'El Gibbor* (the mighty god)[13]. Psalms 147:5 states, "Great is our Lord and mighty in power, his understanding has no limit" (NIV). God's greatness and power are beyond our comprehension. Often, we will attest to the Lord's greatness, yet we do not have a strong meaning of the word great. When we use this word as an adjective, it refers to several meanings. God is great means that He is unlimited; immeasurable is his power. He is vast, suggesting that our Lord is everywhere; there is no escaping him. Our Lord is celebrated, which signifies his mighty characteristics. For those who encounter his excellence, they praise and worship his acts. Our Lord is noble and heroic, for He is strong in battle and never lost a war. God is a highly excellent being who reigns in greatness because of his almighty stature.

Thinking of his greatness leads us to one of God's most known names, *'El Shaddai*, the Almighty God[14]. *'El Shaddai* is used throughout the Old Testament as a tribute to God's mighty power. It is also a testament to God being the sovereign ruler of all. God first revealed his name to Abram when He made his covenant with him (Gen 17:1). Later, this name would appear forty-eight times within Abraham, Isaac, and Jacob's patriarchal age. Describing God as almighty means that He is "all-sufficient," eliminating any other god being mightier than our Lord.

Analyzing the name *'El Shaddai*, we will find several root words that ultimately distinguish God as more than enough. We have established that

---

12. "Names of God," line 22.
13. "Hebrew Names." line 75.
14. "Hebrew Names," line 74.

el is descriptive of God's strength, power, and might; however, the next Hebrew term in 'El Shaddai is "Shad," which means "breast."[15] This word seems misplaced when discussing a God of strength and power. Yet, in the natural, mammals' breasts are a source of nourishment to feed their young. Therefore, God is the supreme nourisher who supplies us with the substance of his Word. By his Word, we are made strong. In First Peter 2:2, Peter believed that we should crave after God as newborn babies desire the milk from their mothers' breasts. Within this notion, God shows that we do not have to yearn for anything of this world because He is our mighty supplier.

In Isaiah 40:11, it states, "He shall feed his flock like a shepherd: he shall gather the lambs with his arm, and carry them in his bosom…" The Bosom of God carries us like a mother who takes her young or like a shepherd who carries a delicate lamb. As a child runs into his mother's bosom for comfort, we as the children of the Most High God can run to him. God's bosom protects us, and we can rest in his reassurance.

Psalm 84:11 states, "For the Lord God is a sun and shield; The Lord gives grace and glory; No good thing does he withhold from those who walk uprightly." Scripturally demonstrating God's sufficiency towards his people. When we feel defeated, he can be a "life-giving source" like the sun, or when we need protection, He can be a shade like a shield. The Bosom of God provides comfort through his divine supplications as our every need is met through him.

"Dai" is the next Hebrew root word that means "pours out."[16] Envision a pitcher of water being poured out into an empty glass. The water makes an impact and starts to fill the cup continuing its flow until it reaches the brim, and the water starts overflowing. Even after the pitcher is empty, the access water continues to move on the surface. Now imagine Acts 2:17, as God pours out his spirit on all flesh. We merely are empty vessels waiting for the spirit of God to impact our lives, filling our cups. God's spirit continues to pour out until it reaches an overflow, which continues to move over the surface of his people. However, unlike the pitcher, the living water of God never empties and never runs dry.

The notion that God pours out on us is demonstrated in Isaiah 44:3–4. Within these Scriptures, God speaks to Jacob, stating that He would pour water out on the thirsty and bring floods on drylands. Just like the

---

15. "The Meaning," line 8.
16. "Names of God," line 3.

Samaritan woman at the well, God will meet our spiritual thirst with everlasting water. Drylands are often cracked with little signs of conservation or life. Symbolically, God restoring the drylands is likened to God stating that He will reestablish everything dry or desolate in our lives to bring forth spiritual and natural existence.

Within the context of Malachi 3:10, God states in his word that he will pour out blessings if we render unto him what is his. In the world of finance, there is a saying which states, "pay yourself first,[17]" which is to say invest in yourself before you pay anything else. However, the best investment a Christian can make is giving their tithes to God. Tithes often is a heated debate in some churches as they do not understand the blessings in giving. God is so gracious that He allows us to keep 90 percent of our earnings. On top of this, he promises to pour out so many blessings that we will not have room enough to receive. These are the provisions that God makes for those who obey his word.

Shaddai combines the two terms "shad" and "dai," which ultimately means one who supplies or one who provides[18]. The impact of this definition shows that God is equipped to bless his people. God's blessings are not merely accessible; however, they will chase us down. His provisions are endless as he gives to the just as well as the unjust. He provides the same sunshine, rain, and breath of life to all his creation regardless of their standing in him. However, for believers, the blessings of God will overtake us if we abide by his sovereign will (Deut 28:2).

His sovereign will have been classified as the "hidden will of God.[19]" Often, Christians are afraid to surrender their wills to God because it is unknown territory. We understand that God is Almighty, yet we do not want to yield to his commands. His hidden will can be likened to a dark place as we desperately search for light to see the mysteries surrounding us. God said that He would be a lamp for our feet and a light for our path (Ps 119:105), which means we can trust his plan. Seeking the blind yes from his people seems a lot to ask; however, this is testing our faith. As Christians, we must realize that light always overpowers darkness. The Almighty God will not leave us in the shadows of fear and doubt but will guide us to his perfect will because of his divine grace and mercy.

---

17. Kagan, "Pay Yourself First," line 3.
18. Parson, "The Name 'El Shaddai,'" line 14.
19. Sproul, "The Will of God," line 3.

God is a merciful god despite creation being unworthy of compassion. Nevertheless, He is '*El Rachum*, the God of Mercy[20]. Mercy is the act of providing forgiveness despite having the authority and power to correct it. Our God is rich in mercy, and He showers this gift on us daily. Without his grace, it would be impossible to live. However, because of his great love for us, we can obtain the richness of his compassion and his understanding. The fact of the matter is that we have done nothing in which God should show us mercy; however, we are saved only because of it (Titus 3:5). Despite our wrongdoings, he delights in showing us compassion. Our Lord understands that we all have sinned and come short of his glory, yet he has freely given us mercy through his Son Jesus Christ (Rom 3:23–24).

There was a no more generous act of sympathy as when God gave his only begotten Son to die for our sins. Through the blood of Jesus, we have been able to gain the mercy of salvation. For this cause, God also asks his children to show forth mercy to one another. Mercy is so critical that we should "bind it around our neck and write it on the tablets of our hearts" (Prov 3: 3–4). By doing so, we will be able to gain favor with God as well as man. In all honesty, as God's creation, we did not deserve mercy. We were unworthy of the cross. However, God continuously shows us his compassion. He knew his creation would not be perfect; however, the mercy of God keeps us in his glory.

God is '*El Hakkavod*, the God of Glory[21]. In the final chapter of Psalms, the writer tells us to "praise God in the firmament of his power, for his mighty acts, as well as for his excellent greatness" (Ps 150:1–2). Unbelievers may wonder why we praise God; however, these Scriptures demonstrate that he has shown himself worthy of praise. It appears that the glory of God is indeed the great move of God's spirit. One of the most astonishing accomplishments of his glory is when his son became flesh. "And the Word became flesh, and dwelt among us, and we saw his glory, glory as of the only begotten from the Father, full of grace and truth" (John 1:14). Throughout the Bible, we can attest to the mighty acts God displayed from the time of the creation to the resurrection. Amazingly, God's power is not limited to only biblical accounts, but his glory continues to flow even today.

God's glory sometimes is challenging to understand because it's used as both a noun and a verb. The noun definition reflects one who has honor gained by noteworthy triumphs and something of great beauty. Seeing that

---

20. "'El Rachum," line 2.
21. "Forty-four El Names," line 14.

EL

God is the most glorious being in all the earth, he loved us so that he placed us in his image. Only because of his mercy can we be image-bearers of his glory, being seen as beautiful instead of unsightly. Despite the evil that we commence, he still covers us with his glory, beautifying us with salvation.

The glory of God is indeed the splendor of his majesty. On one occasion, David said he wanted to behold the Lord's beauty and inquire in his temple (Ps 27:4). Even though no one has seen God, David counted him as beautiful. Indeed, the Lord's ways are wonderful; however, the beauty of God is the reserved qualities that are his alone. As we have studied, God is omnipotent, omnipresent, and omniscient; He is all. However, He is also infinite, without measure, as well as holy without flaw. God is sovereign and self-sufficient, only relying on his divine spirit, which is without physical form. The glory of God is the transfiguration of the bad qualities of sin to the most beautiful attributes of God's spirit (2 Cor 3:18). Therefore, when God said, "let us make man in our own image," perhaps He was speaking of the attributes of himself, man could possess, such as love, joy, gentleness, and goodness (Gal 5:22–23).

The verb definition of glory means "worshipful praise, honor, and thanksgiving." We have learned that everything with breath can praise God; however, worship is reserved for those who have a close relationship with him. Giving God a "worshipful praise" appears to be the next level of admiration for the Father. Praise and worship are not as continuous as giving God glory. Throughout our daily lives, we may praise or worship God; however, establishing God's glory in our lives is an ongoing process as everything we do should glorify his name.

When we glorify God, we must do it in a spirit of truth. True worship equates to a truthful God, *'El Emet*, "the faithful God of Truth."[22] There are times in our lives that we doubt God's words. Our world is filled with atheists who recognize God but do not believe in him. However, are we borderline atheists when we do not stand firm on his promises? Reasonably, there are some things God has spoken to us that have not yet come to pass. God's words are not measured by time, but the truth measures it as every word that is spoken has a purpose and will accomplish that specific task (Isa 55:11).

Isaiah, Jonah, and Nahum all foretold the great fall of the Assyrian empire within one hundred and fifty years. Under King Manasseh's reign, the Israelites committed idolatry against God by restoring the worship of

---

22. "Forty-four El Names," line 6.

Ba'al and the Asherah poles in which his father, King Hezekiah, denounced. Moreover, he even practiced Moloch worship, casting his son into a fiery pit. Due to their wickedness, God stated he would abandon the Israelites and deliver them into their enemies' hands (2 Kgs 21:14). Isaiah prophesied that Assyria would be the "rod of God's anger" to punish the Israelites. However, due to their triumphant boasting, God decided to reprove them as well.

The capital of Assyria was Nineveh, which was called "the bloody city." This moniker was given due to the brutal and torturous acts towards their enemies. Nations feared these gruesome tactics as Assyrian kings would make pyramids of their captives' heads and hang them like ornaments on trees. As a tribute to their incredible power, defeated kings' hands would decorate the empire walls while their discarded bodies would garnish the city gates. This was the pride of the Assyrian empire. There were no other cities like Nineveh, yet Jonah and Nahum prophesied this metropolis's destruction (Nah 2:13).

God had given Nineveh a time to repent through Jonah; however, their repentance was short-lived. Roughly, one hundred and fifty years later, Nahum continuously proclaimed that God was a jealous God (*'El Kanno*); slow to "anger and great in power,"[23] yet there is a time when the wrath of God cannot be stopped (Nah 3:19). Just as Jonah prophesied, Nahum also stated that God would destroy the Assyrian empire by cutting off their pride, Nineveh. Within fifty years, the city of Nineveh was indeed destroyed by the Babylonians.

Despite the time length, God's words must come to pass, which causes God to be *'El Emunah*, translated as the Faithful God[24]. Jonah's prophecy occurred approximately one hundred and fifty years before Nahum's prediction. Both remarkable events demonstrate the real character of God's words as He is faithful and just to keep his promises. Great is the Lord's faithfulness towards his people as He causes the sun to rise and the earth to stand. These are the necessary foundations of his dedication that we disregard as true. However, He has the power to cease the sun from shining and the earth from standing. At God's core, his character is faithful as the Lord keeps his promises and his words towards those that love him (Deut 7:9).

The promises of God cannot be broken because He is holy; He cannot lie. Therefore, our God is *'El Shamar Beriyth*, a God who keeps his

---

23. "Forty-four El Names," line 29.
24. "'El Emunah", line 2.

covenant[25]. Within biblical context, a covenant is an agreement between God and specific individuals. During the old testament, God provided four major promises, which one was the Noahic Covenant. Because sin was prevalent, God decided to destroy the entire world. God caused rain to fall, causing massive destruction over the earth. However, due to Noah's faithfulness, God promised that he would not obliterate the world with water again, sealing it with the sign of the rainbow. These words were spoken thousands of years ago, which is a testament that God keeps his agreements as the earth has withstood floods, tsunamis, and hurricanes, and not once has it been demolished.

Each promise that God gave appears to connect, providing the ultimate redemption. Abraham was promised land and many offspring, in which these offspring would become God's chosen people. Within this covenant, we see that God has established a group of individuals that He has chosen to be his own. Under the Mosaic Covenant, God promised that he would rescue these people, becoming their God, and he would dwell with them forever. He pronounced that Israel would be set apart from any other nation and race of people because they were his chosen. God gave the Israelites the ten commandments along with other laws, which they were to keep. In return, God promised to bless and protect Israel.

Regrettably, the Israelites broke their agreement, and God's favor towards them ceased. Despite this, God was faithful and just, keeping his agreement always coming to their rescue. This is a testament that God never breaks his promises, even though we break our commitment to him. God promised David that He would rule over Israel and all his descendants if they remained faithful to him. God fulfilled all these promises as Abraham's descendants are great in number, Israel is still God's chosen people, and out of David's bloodline came the Savior of the World that will rule forever, delivering us from all sin.

Appreciatively, we are not left out of the promises of God. Within the New Covenant, God promises that He would place his divine Spirit within us and would be faithful to forgive our sins. This promise is sealed by the death and resurrection of his Son, Jesus Christ. Once he died, we were all able to partake of the Spirit of God through the Holy Ghost. No longer were animal sacrifices necessary because God made the ultimate sacrifice. It appears to have provided a redemptive theme of deliverance from sin with

---

25. "Covenant," lines 1–3.

each of the old testament covenants. However, the final part of this plan was Jesus Christ, who would die, providing us with a pathway to salvation.

Frequently, we may wonder if God will remain loyal to his Word. The answer is always yes, as all the promises of God are yes and amen (2 Cor 1:20). The promises of God make him known as '*El Hanne'eman*[26], the faithful God. We have viewed major covenants of God's faithfulness. Yet, in the simplest form, he shows his dedication towards us on an everyday basis. Has there ever been a day that we did not see the sun, or the ocean disappeared? Naturally, we take these things for granted. However, if it had not been for God orchestrating the sun to rise and the water to remain in its place, we would be utterly perplexed. Yet God never goes off duty. He holds the sun in place, allows the stars to brighten the darkness, and even tells the ocean how far to go on land.

Amazingly, God's faithfulness to us is demonstrated continuously as his way is perfect. David spoke of God's perfectness in 2 Sam 22:31, singing, "As for God, his way is perfect the word of the Lord is tried: he is a buckler to all them that trust in him." When David said that the "word of the Lord is tried," this means that he took God at his word. There are times we use a GPS to provide direction to a destination. However, there are times when despite having this device, we ignore the instructions. For whatever reason, we think the GPS is not leading us on the right path. So, we take another route, not knowing that the device is attempting to decrease roadblocks, traffic jams and remove us from accidents along the way. Even though we arrive at our destination, we arrive later because we did not follow the plan.

Often this is how we are with God. He will try to block the obstacles ahead by giving clear instructions, yet we disregard them because we may not understand the way. However, wholly trusting in God will get us to our destination. Becoming off course by leaning on our understanding will derail the straight path God has provided for us. Yet, if we follow God's perfect system (GPS), it will always direct us despite the faced barriers.

When traveling, there are times we may follow the GPS; however, we still experience challenges. We have a flat tire, we lose signal, or there is inclement weather. So, it is with God's way. He never said that his way would be easy. He told us that He would try us (I Pet 4:12). However, this does not mean that God's way is not still perfect. When these challenges arise, David said that God is a buckler for him. A buckler is a portable shield that protects the entire body during battle. David's comparison to God being a

---

26. "Names of God," line 20.

buckler means that 1) we can take God wherever we go, and 2) God is our total covering during life's tests. We must encounter all challenges that God lays before us as faithful Christians to endure our faith's trying.

In 2 Samuel 22:33, David says that God is his strength and power, making his way perfect. King David was a great soldier who won many battles over the Philistine. His exploits were known among all nations, yet David knew the source of his strength did not come from his abilities but God's. God is '*El Mauz*, God of Strength[27] and '*El Chayil* God of Power[28]. In Second Corinthians 12:9, Jesus said that his strength and power are made perfect in our weaknesses. David was the runt of the litter of Jesse's sons. He was not the strongest, nor was he the mightiest. His disposition was not of a great warrior, who is strong and courageous, but of a gentle and meek shepherd. God used David's inadequate appearance to make him one of the greatest warriors capturing over 1000 chariots, 7000 chariot drivers, and 20,000 soldiers and killing over 22,000 Arameans. This is a testament to how God will produce supernatural strength into a weakened vessel.

Our diminished state is an opportunity for God to prove his divine power. David was a great warrior only because he had a significant number of enemies. Allowing continued strength in us is a recipe for a weakened believer as we may begin to rely on our capabilities and resources. For this cause, the Bible instructs us to "be strong in the Lord and the power of his might" (Eph 6:10). It does not tell us to rely on our strength as we have no strength of our own. All of our strength comes from God (Jer 9:23–24). If David never became a weakened vessel, then God could never pour his eternal strength into him.

Trials and tribulations come to strip us from preconceived sources of strength. David's fictitious strength could have been in his status as well as his family. Many times, we will rely on our position or our family members as a resource of strength. However, God will remove those sources until we are entirely dependent upon him. David had status with King Saul as he served him well, yet this same man sought his life on numerous occasions. Absalom was King David's son, which David loved with all his heart. However, his son undermined his authority, seeking after his kingship. With all his sources being stripped, David realized that his strength had to come from God during these challenging times.

---

27. "Forty-Four El Names," line 25.
28. Francis, "Chayil Glory", lines 1–5.

When God strengthens, all we must do is rest on his strength while he goes into battle for us. God is *El Nathan*, the Lord avenges us[29]. Even though God will often disrobe us from our sources, He will shield us from the battle as the battle is not ours but his (2 Chr 20:15). David's enemies came from within his inner circle. This betrayal hurt as many times in Psalms we see his songs of praise, but we can testify to his songs of sadness.

Nevertheless, David understood God to be his strength, rock, and fortress in which he could take shelter during these difficult times. Despite having opportunities to avenge himself, David allowed God to do the retaliating. Vengeance occurred at the Battle of Mount Gilboa when Saul fell on his sword, committing suicide to avoid being captured by the Philistines (I Sam 31:4). Even though David was supposed to fight that day, he did not have to draw his sword as God avenged him.

God's vengeance came against Absalom as he revolted against his father. More importantly, he went against God's chosen vessel. Even our bloodline does not matter to God. If we are the chosen property of the Lord, then everyone must handle us with care. Ironically, Absalom probably only saw his father, the king, instead of seeing David's true position as a child of God. David was the chosen king of Israel, and Absalom had the audacity not to undermine his father but to undermine God. Even though David did not want his son to be harmed, this was his fate. David had to realize that even though this was his son, he attempted to derail God's plans, causing him now to be God's enemy. Unfortunately, for Absalom, no enemy of God has lived as the Lord said in his word, vengeance is mine, and I shall repay (Deut 32:35).

It is easy for us to feel like we must avenge ourselves when God's ears seem deaf to our sorrow. However, God is *El Shama*, a God who hears[30]. When being pursued by King Saul, David prayed to the Lord that he would listen to him during one of the lowest points of his life (Ps 17:6). David could have easily killed Saul; however, David decided to have a conversation with God. He knew that God's ears were inclined to his cry for help. God's ears are still listening to the moans of his people. The Lord tells us to call upon him when we are in trouble, and he will deliver us from them all (Ps 50:15). This is yet another promise that God gives to the righteous. If we call upon the name of the Lord, he will indeed hear our cry.

---

29. "El Nathan," line 2.
30. "El Shama," lines 9-10.

EL

In Psalms 42, the sons of Korah called on the Lord's name as they longed for God. These men came from the genealogy of Korah, who was killed because he challenged Moses and Aaron (Num 16:28–35). However, despite their ancestor's disloyalty, they were spared and became devoted worshippers of God. As the psalm continues, the sons of Korah believed God to be '*El Yeshuah*, the God of my salvation'[31] and '*El Sela*, God my rock'[32]. God indeed saved their lives as He could have easily destroyed them. However, God spared the lineage, and these men became great choral leaders for King David at a devastating point in his life.

During this time, David's daughter was raped by his son Ammon. Absalom, his son, killed Ammon, and his trusted servants killed Absalom for his attempt to overthrow the kingdom. Not only this, but the king's grieving was met with disdain and ridicule. This sign of weakness would later cause other nations to mock King David and Israel. To say that he was depressed is an understatement as he was emotionally defeated. However, the sons of Korah wrote Psalms 42 and 43 to describe David's plight, but also to remind him that his hope is in the Lord.

Clinging on our hope in God seems like the only thing we can do during trials and tribulations. Even though King David seemed hopeless, he also knew God as '*El lemosha'oth*, God of his deliverance'[33]. On several occasions, David experienced great divine delivering power of the Almighty. David decided to prove God's word as he understood that He previously delivered him from a lion, delivered him from a bear, and knew that God would deliver him from the Philistines. God not only delivered him from his enemy but even allowed him to live peacefully among them. David said that the Lord prepares a table before him among his enemies, and his cup runs over (Ps 23:5). This is a testament to how God can and will deliver us. Amazingly God, will not only allow us to escape our problem, but he will let what we feared to become a base for our victory.

One of the most significant signs of victory and deliverance occurred while the Israelites were enslaved in Egypt. Four hundred years were the people of God subjugated to the Egyptians. Ironically, it seems farfetched to believe that God's people were imprisoned by those who believed in pagan gods. However, this was the plight that the Israelites found themselves in due to disobedience. Yet, God was able to deliver his chosen people from

---

31. "Forty-four El Names," line 27.
32. "Forty-four El Names," line 22.
33. "God of Deliverances," lines 10–12.

Pharaoh as well as the wilderness. Ten plagues came upon Egypt to set God's people free, yet once God freed them, they spent another forty years enslaved in the Zin Desert due to unbelief. However, the good news is that there was still victory within the wilderness.

There are Christians today who are freed but imprisoned by their disbelief. God punished the Israelites because of disobedience and their lack of faith in him to give them the land of their inheritance. Today, we have believers who have been set free from sin but entangled with the vines of disbelief.

Hearing the word "wilderness," we often think of a horrible place, not fit for dwelling. If that was the case, then why did the Israelites take forty-years to leave? If we google pictures of the wilderness, we will see beautiful pastures, mountains, and trees. Spiritually, this is how our wilderness appears. As God still provides just as he did with the Israelites, we are magnificently comfortable with our surroundings. They may not have had all they wanted, but it was better than nothing. This notion is still like our own today. We rather live contentedly in the wilds instead of pursuing the journey that God has for us. It was not God's intent for his people to live in the wilderness, as God does not intend for us to stay comfortable within his provisions. Each of us has a God-given destination. However, it is our choice if we want to remain in the wasteland or pursue our victory.

Before God even delivered the Israelites from Kadesh Barnea, the Lord gave instructions concerning their success. God spoke to Moses regarding how the people should atone for their sins while they were still captive in the wilderness (Lev16). God could have easily waited until they were released from the desert, but truthfully, God had already seen them dwelling in the promised land. Often, God will keep us in a place of discomfort to bring overwhelming deliverance in our lives. The desert was unpleasant, but God had already provided their rescue from the dry place. As Christians, even if we find ourselves in a difficult position, we must wait on his deliverance, knowing that victory is on the other side of the desert.

The wilderness can be an uncomfortable comfortable state in which God wants to remove us from our comfort zone to produce victory. At times, we become too relaxed in God's provisions. However, God calls us out of our secure state to fully trust in him. Abraham, who was known as the Father of Faith, allowed God to lead him blindly (Gen 12:1–2, 4). Indeed, this act of faith was unsettling for Abraham. Nevertheless, his unnerving wilderness state produced a great victory from God (Gen 13: 14–17). The

Lord had promised to give him land, but also to make him a great nation. This was difficult to believe because the odds that Abraham would produce children with his wife Sarai were slim to none. After all, both were old, and naturally, Sarai could not conceive due to her age. Like Abraham and Sarai, we see the obstacles that we face against the promises of God. However, we must stand firm on his promises of victory.

Indeed, God will give us unconceivable promises which seem far-fetched and impossible, yet we must wait on God. Unfortunately, Sarai took matters into her own hands, allowing Abraham to have a child with Hagar, her Egyptian servant. Sarai begins to become jealous of Hagar, oppressing her, she ran away. While Hagar fled, the angel of the Lord asked Hagar to return to Sarai for her child would also be blessed. Hearing this, Hagar stated, "You are the God who sees me," for she said, "I have now seen the One who sees me." (Gen 16:13 NIV). *El Roi* [34] is a God who sees us when we are in despair. Hagar was the least of them; however, God cared about her just as he cared about Abraham and Sarai.

Sarai clearly did not trust God and took matters into her own hand, attempting to ensure God and Abraham's covenant. Even though God told the couple that they would have a child, both doubted the plan as she was ninety years old, and Abraham was one hundred. Even after Sarai doubted God, He still wanted to bless her and Abraham with the child to bring forth nations. This should have been a time to rejoice; instead, Sarai and Abraham decided to laugh (Gen 17:15-21). At this point, it would have been reasonable for God to bless Abraham's son, Ishmael, versus having Sarai produce a child. After all, she had attempted to hurry the plan of God as well as distrust in his Word. Nevertheless, God still wanted to keep the covenant that He had between them to bring forth a child that would begin Israel's great nation.

God is *'El Nahsah*, a God who forgives[35]. An ongoing debate has occurred to determine if doubting God is a sin. Yet, in this incident, God indeed pardoned Abraham and Sarai's lack of trust in him. Not only this, but God pardon Sarai's attempt to aid his promise. God could have easily allowed another couple to bring forth his chosen people, yet He kept His promise and forgave them of their mistrust. The fact that God was still gracious to them is a testament to how his forgiveness brings forth change in our lives. Even during their doubt, God produced a shift within their lives,

---

34. "Hebrew Names," line 94.
35. "Beautiful Names," line 33.

changing Abraham's wife's name from Sarai to Sarah to become a "mother of nations." Despite their skepticism, God kept his word, forgiving them of their doubt and distrust in him.

Incredibly, God is an all-knowing being. He is omniscient; however, the only thing that He will forget is our past sins (Isa 43:25). Once we repent, God forgives our sins and will not hold us accountable. He will throw them behind His back (Isa 38:17), blot them out (Isa 44:22), remember them no more, (Heb 8:12), and will cast them in the depth of the sea (Mic 7:19). God's plan of forgiveness started long ago despite our continued wrongdoings. Instead of dealing with us harshly, he provided his Son, Jesus Christ, who bore our sins on the cross and covered them with His blood (Eph 1:7). When the blood of Jesus poured out, every sin we ever or will commit was covered and rescinded because of his death.

God is a gracious God, *'El Channun*[36]. Amazingly, despite our ongoing disobedience and doubt, the Lord longs to be generous to his children (Isa 30:18). Psalm 111:4 says that God is full of compassion. His stature is immeasurable, which also means that there is no limit to his kindness. As we take inventory of our lives, we can attest to the many counts of misconduct we committed against God. Continual sin should have equaled immediate death; our fate should have been fatal, but God longed to show everlasting grace. Our God is merciful, gracious, slow to anger, and is plenteous in mercy (Ps 103:8). Even though we do not deserve the blessings of God, He continues to shower down his grace and mercy within our lives.

After the Lord had delivered the Israelites from the wilderness, their behavior seemed oblivious to God's sovereignty. He had proved himself, and despite witnessing the Almighty's power, they returned to worshipping pagan gods (2 Kgs 17:7–17). The Israelites began to build images, placing them on every high hill and under every tree to worship. Ironically, they made a terrible grievance against the Lord, placing idols on the land he gave them. Imagine how God felt after choosing these people to be his elected people to witness them set-up, false gods.

Before the Israelites had committed sins against God, and it may have appeared that He was slow to react. However, within this text, we see that idolatry had provoked the Lord's anger. Due to their disobedience and acts of sin, the Lord removed Israel from his sight, causing them to become captive by Assyria and even allowing lions to devour several Israelites (2 Kgs 17:23, 25). God is slow to anger; however, we should not antagonize

---

36. "Forty-four El Names," line 20.

him. He may not necessarily allow a country to attack or a beast to destroy. Nonetheless, we may be consumed by oppression, failure, or fear. Even though God is slow to anger, we should not incite him with continued immorality but continuously follow his creed.

Even in the midst of our sins, the Most High God, *'El Elyon*[37], wants to have a relationship with his children. The prophet Malachi wanted to restore this relationship that God once had with the Israelites. However, after being delivered from Babylonia, the people continued to sin against God. It appeared that their desire for him had waxed cold as they forgot how he delivered them from captivity. Instead of returning to God's law, they began to participate in intermarriages (Mal 2:10). The prophets of old warned the Israelites not to take foreign wives, yet the relationship was broken as the Israelite men sought after pagan women.

This seems to foreshadow what is currently happening in the church today. Christian believers are committing adultery, divorcing God, and having relationships with ungodly principles and doctrines. God forewarns that we should not have other gods as He is the Highest God, which means that He is the greatest in all the universe. Frequently, people will commit infidelities as they search for something better. Since our Lord has supreme jurisdiction over all life and has been deemed the Highest God, there is nothing superior to his stature. Nevertheless, we are still unfaithful to him.

Paul admonished believers that we should not be unequally yoked with unbelievers (2 Cor 6:14–16). A yoke is utilized between two animals to help pull weight. If the oxen are unequally yoked, this means that they are not equal in size or strength. Christians being bound together with unbelievers is not an equivalent relationship as the stronger will draw the weaker. We are surrounded by those who do not believe in Christian principles; therefore, it would be ludicrous to think we will not have contact with unbelievers. Yet, this does not mean that we should pursue relationships with them. Entering associations with them is the same notion that God forewarned the Israelites about intermarriages.

Paul continues his teachings by saying, "what fellowship does the righteous have with the unrighteous"? God is a righteous God, *'El Tsaddik*[38], who entreats righteousness within his children because we are his likeness. The righteousness of God is a standard of being "morally justifiable" in action and deed. One of God's most prominent characteristics

---

37. "Forty-four El Names," line 9.
38. "Forty-four El Names," line 7.

is giving us a blueprint on how to seek our righteousness. We have been made the righteousness of God through and by the death of his Son, Jesus Christ (2 Cor 5:21). Transforming from immorality to morality could only occur through a righteous being, who never knew sin, but became sin for us. Through the covering of our sins, our righteousness was revealed and manifested in him, yet if we associate with unbelievers, our lives may become tainted again with iniquity.

Second Corinthians 6:17 tells us that we should separate from the unrighteous if we want to be welcomed by Christ. It is exceedingly rare to see two species of birds interacting with one another as "birds of a feather, flock together." Likewise, those who are yoked with Christ should follow those who are righteous. In chapter 15 of the first book of Corinthians, Paul was teaching about the resurrection of Jesus Christ. Many Jewish believers did not believe this notion and attempted to teach against the truth. However, Paul admonished Corinth's church to depart from poor company as they will corrupt their lives with evil. Associating with individuals who are not followers of Christ will attempt to persuade moral judgment unless they walk by the Spirit (Gal 5:16). Within the last days, the unrighteous will inherit death as the righteous will inherit the kingdom of God (Eph 5:5). Therefore, as the righteous of God, we should protect our inheritance against those who attempt to steal our righteousness.

Being the righteous of God means that we are blameless as God, himself, is blameless. There is no sin in God, neither is he a man that can be made to sin. His stature is perfect, pure, and holy. Therefore, his virtue withstands all the world's depravities. As the body of Christ, he calls us to be righteous. All have sinned and fallen short of the glory of God. Nevertheless, through the shedding of his precious blood, we can now have a relationship with the one that formed us.

In Isaiah 43:1–3, God tells the Israelites that He is the one that formed them as He called them by his name. Being called by God means that He calls us to righteous living, and in return, He will guide us through life's tribulations. Within these verses, He retells the miracles performed as the Israelites walked through the water and did not get wet. Or when Shadrach, Meshach, and Abednego went through the fire, they were not burnt. Remarkably, *'El Chuwl*, the One that formed thee[39], will cover us through life's fiery trials and will be a life "Savior" to keep us from drowning. As the

---

39. "Beautiful Names," line 21.

EL

righteous of God, we will go through trials and tribulations, but since his grace covers us, we will not look like what we have been through.

Awesome is the Lord our God, *'El Hanna*[40], who can keep us in times of trouble. Several scriptures within the Bible verbalize God as being terrible. We know this word to take on a negative form, such as dreadful or awful. However, in the biblical text, it shows the greatness of God, which is awe-inspiring. In Psalm 47:2 it states, "For the Lord most high is terrible, he is a great King over all the earth." This seems contradictory as one part describes him as horrible, yet another says He is magnificent. As dialects changed, the root word of terrible means "awesome and great." Therefore, many newer translations of the Bible use the word awesome to describe the Lord.

God is truly an awesome God, as everything that He does is tremendous. His love is overwhelming, his mercy and grace are magnificent, his power is overcoming; he is perfect and just in all his ways, and his faithfulness to us is remarkable (Deut 32:4). There is no one like our God. He is God alone who made the heavens and their host, the earth, and the sea and all that is in it. Even the host of heavens worships him (Neh 9:6). He is so awesome that every word he speaks must come to pass as his awesomeness will not allow him to lie (Num 23:19). He is a God that keeps His promises to his children. He is the sovereign God that formed the light and created the darkness, who also makes calm and calamity, which signifies His power and dominion in all the earth. He is terrific in all his ways, with none matching His power within all the universe (Isa 45:7).

He is the great king who will reign from everlasting to everlasting (Isa 43:13), which causes him to be *'El Olam*, the everlasting God[41]. There is no beginning or end to him. Ironically, we live our lives based upon time. The hours we work, the hours we sleep, the days we have off. Calendars and dates consume us. However, imagine a world not based upon time, a place with an incalculable existence where calendars and clocks cease to exist. Our humanistic mindset may not allow us to comprehend a place where time is nonexistent. Yet, heaven will be a place where we will be able to dwell with the everlasting God for eternity. There will be no need for time as we will be with the eternal God, who could simply pause the clock and let time standstill.

---

40. "Forty-four El Names," line 30.
41. "Names of God," line 24.

God is an awesome God because He is immeasurable. There is no way that we can measure eternity, nor can we predict the age of God. Before God created anything, He existed in time even when there were no time intervals. He had to develop it before it could exist. God tells us in his word that his timetable is different than ours as one day is a thousand years to him (2 Pet 3:8). If we attempt to calculate seconds to minutes, one second is approximately 144,000 minutes or 100 days to God. Hilariously, many of us believe we have been waiting for a long time on God's blessings when the years equal a few seconds for God. God has already performed what we have asked and has moved on to the next blessing He has in store.

Before the beginning of time, the Lord chose us and already knew what we would need before we could even ask (Eph 1:4). Imagine, God knew our names, who we would be, and even where we would live before he even created the place we would dwell. God consecrated his beloved, setting us apart while we were merely forming in our mother's womb (Jer 1:5). As Jesus prayed the high priestly prayer, he indicates that God glorified and loved him before the world was even fashioned (John 17). Amazingly, this love that God had for his Son foreshadowed the love that God would have for us before we even existed.

Since God saw us before time, he also knew the trials we would face and the sins that we would commit. Gratefully, to redeem us from the hands of death, he sent his incarnate Son to die for our iniquities; *Immanuel*, God with us[42]. Immanuel was only mentioned three times in the Bible, spoken first by the prophet Isaiah proclaiming that a Savior shall be born of a virgin birth (Isa 7:14). This Savior would be God the Son who would provide the ultimate sacrifice and surrender all for his creation to restore us from sin.

In Genesis 6:6, God repented that he even made man, as the creation he loved continuously sinned against him. God's mighty power could have eradicated humanity. However, God had a contingency plan in his Son. God, the Son, saw the grief that his father was enduring and said, "Prepare me a body, and I will go down to redeem man" (Heb 10:4–7). Despite being equal to God, Jesus took on the form of his creation, surrendering everything to become a curse (Phil 2:6–8). Imagine God preparing his own body to redeem man. Therefore, when Isaiah prophesied that the Messiah would be called Immanuel, the prophecy became literal as God was with them walking on the Earth.

---

42. "Names of God," line 24.

EL

Typically, we do not consider what Jesus genuinely gave up for us when he came to this world. We often give praise for his death, but we must consider his life. For thirty-three years, Jesus was imprisoned on this earth subjected to laws and rules despite being the Son of God. He was on death row, being born to die, denouncing his divine right to act and behave like God. Not only this, but Jesus left his rightful place seated on the right hand of his Father. A place that all Christians are striving to be, he merely left that we may have the right to the Kingdom of God. Imagine being in the presence of the Lord before the beginning of time and now leaving that glory behind. Jesus surrendered his relationship with his Father to redeem us through the death of the cross. The fact is that Jesus died to save man, but for thirty-three years, he also suffered and lived for us as well.

Even today, Emmanuel continues to be with us as we are the temple of God (1 Cor 3:16). Through the Holy Spirit, we still have a connection with the Almighty God. As Jesus warned the disciples of the hardship to come, they became sorrowful. It was difficult to hear that they would be hated among men and put to death because of him. However, he said He would not leave them but will be with them always, sending them the Comforter, the Holy Ghost. Once again, signifying that God was still with them and continues to be with us.

God has ordained us to be powerful and courageous in the power of his might (Josh 1:9). Even though we may face difficult challenges, we have the ability that resonates within us because of his Spirit. In studying the name El, we can attest to the many Scriptures that have demonstrated that our God is immeasurable and limitless throughout the world. Simply put, our God is ruler and creator of all; there is nothing more significant than him. Since He is the highest authority, we should not be dismayed or afraid. His name alone means power as He is the sovereign ruler and omnipotent authority within the Heavens and the earth: "El," "the strong controller of all."

Chapter 3

YHVH or YAHWEH

And God said unto Moses, I AM THAT I AM: and he said, Thus shalt thou say unto the children of Israel, I AM hath sent unto you.

Exodus 3:14

YHVH ALSO KNOWN AS the "Tetragrammaton"[1], is the Hebrew name in which God revealed to Moses at Mount Horeb (Exod 3:15). *HaShem*, "The Name"[2] or *Shem Hameforash*, "the Special Name,"[3] are also titles referencing this holy moniker. YVHH was deemed so sacred that Jewish believers forbade it to be spoken aloud, thus losing proper pronunciation[4]. Some biblical scholars believed that the Israelites did this following God's commandment, "thou shalt not speak the name of the Lord in vain."[5] Nevertheless, the articulation of YVHH has since become "*Yahweh*"[6] or "*Jehovah*."[7] In the Bible, the capitalization of "LORD" is also known as YVHH[8]. Today, many

---

1. Roat, "What is the Tetragrammaton," line 4.
2. Roat, "What is the Tetragrammaton," line 21.
3. "What is the Tetragrammaton," lines 2–3.
4. "What is the Tetragrammaton," lines 9–11.
5. Roat, "What is the Tetragrammaton," lines 22–25.
6. Roat, "What is the Tetragrammaton," lines 26-27.
7. Roat, "What is the Tetragrammaton," lines 38-40.
8. Roat, "What is the Tetragrammaton," lines 46-50.

YHVH or YAHWEH

Rabbis also use the name *Adonai*, which can be found in the Bible as "Lord," coming from the Ugaritic word, Adon, meaning lords, master, or father[9].

Adon is a root word meaning "to rule[10]," as Adonai signifies that our Lord has rule over the earth. Within this rule, God has the responsibility to protect, guide, and provide for his creation as a master with this title would do for his subjects. Within the Bible, David and Elisha were also given this name to show their leadership over the Israelites (I Sam 24:8, 2 Sam 3:21, and 2 Kgs 2:19). Despite some referring to them as lord or master, we understand that this name, though not exclusive to God, is more of a name that describes who he is within creation. God has been deemed Lord of all Lords, wholly showing forth his rule over every natural ruler. Despite David and Elisha being referred to by this name, God is distinguished as the one Lord of Host.

In Deuteronomy 10:17, it states that God is God of gods and Lord of lords. Some may argue that God and Lord are interchangeable and undisputedly similar in definition, which is relatively accurate. However, they are comparatively spiritually different. It has been established that God is the Supreme Being and Creator. However, the term Lord references that he also can have control and rule over creation. When God fashioned the earth, we had no choice in the matter. He did not reason or consult us in developing the world, thus displaying his sovereign authority. Nevertheless, even though he is Lord, we have this choice to choose to follow him or to deny his rule within our lives (Josh 24:15). As Lord, He has granted free course to declare him as Lord or reject him, ironically, giving us free will to choose.

As the name God, Elohim is the plural of El, so is the name Lord, Adonai, the plural of Adon[11]. Previously analyzing the pluralization of El, Adonai could also reference the sovereign rule of the Holy Trinity as each has been decreed as lord. God established himself as master over the Israelites as He prepared Moses for their deliverance (Exod 6:2). For over four hundred years, the people of God had been enslaved by Pharaoh. They had become accustomed to recognizing Pharaoh's rule over them. This notion was embedded as they were slaves, and he was the supreme ruler within Egypt. However, God reminded the Israelites that even Pharaoh's power did not supersede his authority. It was vital for them to know that God is the creator, but He also has rule over his creation, confirming his lordship.

9. "Hebrew Names of God," lines 1–5.
10. "What is the meaning of Adonai?" lines 3–4.
11. "Hebrew Names of God," lines 6–14.

As Christians, when we accept Jesus Christ as Lord, it means that there is no longer our will, but the will of him whom we follow (Mark 8:34). This is the choice that separates Christians from unbelievers because we deny ourselves, pick up our cross, and follow him (Matt 16:24). Denying ourselves signifies that Jesus has complete jurisdiction over our lives while taking our cross shows our voluntary will to suffer for his name's sake. Our choice to follow him is paid with the gift of salvation (Rom 10:9). Unfortunately, not all of God's creation declares his Son as Lord. However, their confessions will be made known as every knee will bow and acknowledge that he is indeed Lord over all (Phil2: 10–11).

Within the Nicene Creed, the Holy Spirit is deemed "Lord, the Giver of Life[12]." Many believers often do not refer to this part of the Holy Trinity as Lord; however, ironically, the Holy Spirit is the one who controls and regulates our thoughts and behaviors. In having the Spirit of God dwelling within us, we give him control, power, and authority to guide and lead within our lives. Without the Spirit, we would follow behind our understanding without the Holy Ghost's junction, leading us like a master leads his subjects. Therefore, even though we may not call the Holy Spirit Lord, he is the pure definition as he controls and rules to ensure our place in God.

God established his name as YHVH deriving from the Hebrew verb "to be." Other scholars believe that its origins also mean "He-Who-Is."[13] The literary term "be" is a verb that circumferences past, present, and future tense. Therefore, when God fashioned his name, he recognized himself as the eternal being. Before anything, there was God. He is currently here, and he will be present forever. The auxiliary form can be used to "show actions that are in progress,[14]"; meaning that God is always operating. To be is also a linking verb which is the description of someone or something. Consequently, the origins of "He-Who-Is" can also describe God's attributes. *He who is* loving; *He who is* kind, and *He who is* the All-Powerful God. Lastly, the intransitive verb of be means "to exist."[15] Henceforth, establishing that God's existence is endless, it is without a beginning or an end.

The profoundness of God telling Moses, "I AM THAT I AM" was a revelation to God's people. "Ehyeh asher ehyeh" is the phrase that is found

---

12. "Nicene Creed," lines 6–7.
13. "What is the Tetragrammaton" lines 13–15.
14. "The Verb," lines 27–32.
15. "Microsoft Bing Dictionary, line 3.

YHVH or YAHWEH

in Hebrew Bibles meaning "I will be what I will be."[16] This descriptive name of God is displaying God's "self-existence" as well as his immeasurable power to be whatever his people desire him to be within their lives. We can compare this name to a fill-in-the-blank phrase. God says, "I AM THAT I AM" literally means that those who are called by his name can claim God to be whatever they need him to be. As the children of God, all we must do is fill-in-the-blank and God will be what we need him to be at any given point in time.

Throughout the Old Testament, God reveals himself as the "I Am." If we took in context a summary of what God says He is to us, it would read: *I am* El-Shaddai, God Almighty (Gen17:1). Yes, *I am* the Lord, and there is no other Savior (Isa 43:11). *I am* the Lord; that is my name! I will not give my glory to anyone (Isa 42:8). Don't be afraid; *I am* with you. Don't be discouraged, for *I am* your God (Isa 41:10). *I am* merciful (Exod 22:27) and slow to anger, filled with unfailing love and faithfulness (Exod 34:6). *I am* the Lord who heals you (Exod 15:26). *I am* a God who is near (Jer 23:23–24). *I am* the one who comforts you (Isa 51:12). *I am* the Lord, who made all things (Isa 44:24). From eternity to eternity, *I am* God. No one can snatch anyone out of my hand. No one can undo what I have done (Isa 43:13). Remember the things I have done in the past. For I, alone, am God! There is no one like me (Isa 46:9), for *I am* the Lord! If I say it, it will happen (Ezek 12:25) because *I am* the Lord your God (Exod 20:2). This summation is God's undying message to us. It is an invitation of security and reassurance to all of those who believe in his name.

As God was revealed as Lord in the Old Testament, in the New Testament, the Son of God was seen in the same manner. During the infamous foot washing, Jesus said, "You call Me Master and Lord: and you say well; for so *I am*" (John 13:13). Jesus knew his identity as the "Great I am." It was expected that Christ referenced himself as Lord as he merely was taking on the same characteristics as his Father. In the natural, the significance of the surname is to identify and distinguish individuals from each other. When children are born, they usually take on their parents' surname, showing they are identified and recognized as their father's sons or daughters. Therefore, when God declared, "I AM THAT I AM," Jesus took on the Father's name.

Announcing that he is also an "I AM,"; we as the children of God are also the "I am" of God. We, too, have the right to proclaim this name as we are the righteous of God and are joint-heirs with his Son, Jesus Christ

---

16. "The Name of God," lines 2–7.

(Gal 4:7, Rom 8:17). The Word tells us that we are new creatures, giving us the right to say, "*I am* newly restored, *I am* holy, without blame, and *I am* more than a conqueror" (1 Cor 5:17, Eph 1:4, Rom 8:37). Since we can do all things through Christ, we have God's divine permission to use his name according to our faith by proclaiming, "I am healed, I am victorious, I am wealthy, and I am loved." We merely need to understand our God-given right to the name that God has given to his beloved. God is; therefore, *I am*.

Declaring that we are the "I am" of God invites us to learn more about who and what He is Lord over within this realm. Since the name Jehovah means Lord, it has been combined with other Hebrew words to define God's divine lordship from everlasting to everlasting. For example, the name Jehovah has been joined together with the first name of God, Elohim. *Jehovah Elohim* means "The Lord God,[17]" proving that each name has significance and is not as similar as we may once perceive. For example, being a creator of something does not give the inventor control over how an individual chooses to use his invention. The person who invented the butter knife may created it to slice butter, yet another person may use it as a screwdriver. However, God being the Creator and Lord gives him the right to use us as he desires. We may have free will, but God has free course to administer his own sovereign will to utilize his creation for his purpose.

Some names are associated with Jehovah that distinguishes God's ownership within our lives. *Jehovah Eloheenu*, "Lord our God,[18]" is a name that utilizes the word "our," which means "belonging to or associated with[19]." Using this name, we make the declaration that we belong to God and claim to connect to him. *Jehovah Elokehu*, the Lord thy God, and *Jehovah Elohay*, the Lord my God[20], are both names that also claim the acceptance of God as Lord. When using the possessive pronoun "my," it demonstrates ownership. Confessing that God is our Lord indicates that we have an intimate relationship with the divine Creator. We no longer accept the notion that He is merely Lord, but we make it a personal declaration that He is ours.

When we accept God as our Lord, we also freely receive God's benefits. One of those benefits is calling God, *Jehovah Rophe*[21], God our healer, as

---

17. Evans, "Praying and Pronouncing," lines 168–172.
18. "Daily Bible Study," lines 2–4.
19. "Our," lines 1–2.
20. "Daily Bible Study," lines 4–5.
21. "Jehovah's Names," lines 33.

YHVH or YAHWEH

well *as Jehovah Rapha*, the Lord that heals[22]. God promises of healing first appeared in Exodus 15:26, after God freed the Israelites from captivity. God had assured his people that he would not subject them to the infections that came upon the Egyptians with the condition that they listened and obeyed his commandments. This assurance is equivalent to the promises associated with Jesus's agonizing death on the cross. Gratefully, the wounds he took were not in vain as by each stripe we were and are currently healed (Isa 53:5).

Today these promises still ring true. We will be subjected to illness, whether it is a common cold, Covid-19, or cancer. However, if we obey God's word, He promises to heal us from all manner of diseases (Ps 103:3). Through his divine healing power, we are wholly made complete mentally, spiritually, and physically. Even diseases without a current cure or name must come under subjection to God. The only specification that He requires is that we seek his face and turn from our evil ways, and He promises that He will heal our land (2 Chr 7:14–15).

Unfortunately, many do not believe this notion is correct, as several have faced fatality due to physical ailments. Putting into question if God only heals us from sin infirmities or does his power extend to every natural disease? First and foremost, it is vital to understand that being a Christian does not exempt us from sicknesses. However, being a Christian does prevent us from dying a second death (Rev 2:11, 20:6). After Jesus' resurrection, the nail imprints from the crucifixion were still apart of his body. Despite being visible, they were healed, and his body was now made spiritual (1 Cor 15:44). The point is that despite having angels who could have averted his death, Jesus still died. God has charge over every known and unknown disease within this world; however, the notion is that many will still experience terminal illnesses. Yet, just like our Savior's hands, we will be healed as our mortal bodies will take on immortality, never being able to be plagued by disease again.

Psalm 73:26 gives a good illustration of how our natural bodies will fail, but God still heals. Each day our bodies weaken due to age. Naturally, we expect this to occur; however, this psalm says that God will strengthen our hearts, and he is our portion forever. We are two parts: the natural man and the spirit. The first man prepares for death, while the latter prepares for eternal life. The human body is weak and feeble and will be subjected to death, whether due to infection or violent force. However, the spirit man

---

22. Khokhar, "Names for God," line 6.

is strengthened each day by the Word of God. If we abide by God's holy doctrine, our spiritual man grows in strength, preparing itself for immortal existence. Sinful plagues can infect the spiritual man, but thankfully, we have a healer that can restore our divine health.

Another benefit afforded by our Lord is having him as our guide, *Jehovah Rohi*, the Lord is my shepherd[23]. In Psalm 23, David makes this declaration, understanding that we lack absolutely nothing if the Lord is our shepherd. Before David was anointed as the new king of Israel, his job was to tend his father's sheep. Surely, David was thrilled about his new title, however, he was probably more concerned about his unattended sheep. For this cause, it is believed that God counted David as a man of his spirit.

As the shepherd, David's job was to provide a sense of security, protection, restoration, and nutrition for his sheep. God is no different than any good shepherd. Despite having the title of the Almighty God, He looks after his flock. He makes us lie down in green pastures, which overflows with blessings of rest and nutrition. He leads us by the still waters that we may be refreshed and renewed; he guides us on a path of righteousness because he calls us by his name (Ps 23:1–3). When we are weary and faint of heart, he will gather us in His arms and carry us like lambs (Isa 40:11). When the beasts of the field come to kill, steal, and destroy, God, will protect us by his mighty hand (John 10:10). Our good shepherd never comes off duty and provides for our needs to guide and protect his chosen flock.

As our shepherd, God is also our source who has been given the name *Jehovah Jireh*, God, our provider[24]. The first time Abraham revealed this name was during a time in which Abraham's faith was extensively tested. God had requested him to sacrifice his son Isaac (Gen 22). Isaac was the promised son who would bring forth God's chosen nation. Indeed, God had been mistaken in his request as God allowed Abraham and Sarah to have Isaac in their old age. However, nevertheless, Abraham obeyed God and knew that the Lord would provide for the sacrifice. As Abraham prepared to offer his son, a ram in the bush was provided for God's burnt offering.

Through the most challenging times, God will provide for his people. Abraham did not understand the request that God gave to him, but he understood that God is a God that will provide. Even when it seems unbelievable, we must trust that God is the great supplier of all of our needs, even in the direst situations. Food, water, shelter, and protection were all supplied

---

23. Khokhar, "Names for God," line 14.
24. "Jehovah's Names," lines 18.

by God when the Israelites were in the wilderness, and they lacked nothing (Deut 2:7). As long as our God reigns in victory and is rich in glory, He will continually supply our needs. His blessings are infinite; all we must do is deposit belief and praise and watch our investment grow.

God not only provides naturally, but He also provides for us spiritually. God is a provider of sanctification as He is *Jehovah Mekoddishkem*[25], which means "The Lord who sets you apart" or *Jehovah M'Kaddesh*[26], "The One who sanctifies us." When God sanctifies his people, he separates us for a specific duty or task. God set Jeremiah apart before he was even formed in his mother's womb, predestinating he would be a prophet to the nations (Jer 1:5). It's astonishing to think that God sets us apart before we could even become a part of the world. However, he had designated Jeremiah to be his mouthpiece before he was even born. Therefore, God has sanctified us for our specific duties for the uplifting of the kingdom. He has a divine purpose for his entire creation, whether to become a great prophet like Jeremiah or to clean toilets at the church. If that is our assigned duty, we must do our best to perform our tasks despite any barriers or challenges.

One of the challenges that Jeremiah faced was his youth. There has been some debate about the age in which God called Jeremiah, as some believe it was as early as seven or later in early adulthood. However, he was young when God set him apart for the task of speaking against Jerusalem. God will use anyone He sees fit for his divine purpose as God is our creator, *Jehovah Hoseenu*[27]. Jeremiah's age seemed like a hindrance because youth are often underestimated and lack wisdom. However, God knew what Jeremiah was capable of because He was the one that created him. Therefore, God also recognizes our capabilities because He is the one who has equipped us for our designated purpose.

When Henry Ford created the 1908 Model T car, he did not expect this machine to take flight, nor did he think it would sail across seas because this was not its purpose. Our creator will never give us a task that we cannot accomplish because he predestined our talents and gifts before we were even conceived. If God has given us a job, we have been certified as our creator has qualified us for the assignment. The Lord will never give us an impossible mission. For every task that is given to our hands, it is already sealed with the victory. God is our creator who has called us to victorious

---

25. Khokhar, "Names for God," line 10.
26. "Jehovah's Names," lines 22.
27. Khokhar, "Names for God," line 15.

missions. All we must do is "walk worthy of the vocation in which we are called," for he has given us all we need to be successful (Eph 4:1).

God does not merely equip us with what we need to perform the task, but he also guides us through it. He is not a god that would assign a job and then leave us to our own devices. This is not the case as God is *Jehovah Shammah*, The Lord is Present[28]. Ezekiel gave this name to God to exemplify Jerusalem's restoration, but first, he prophesied judgment against Judah and Israel for their wickedness. God gave Ezekiel specific details to accomplish to show the destruction that he would bring to his people. In chapters 4 and 5, God told Ezekiel to do some strange task to act out what would happen to the Israelites. A few of those occurrences were to be bound with rope and lay on his left side for 390 days, representing each year of Israel's sin. Ezekiel then had to lay on his right side for a total of 40 days, demonstrating Judah's immorality. Not only this, but he was given a strict diet of water and bread that was cooked over animal feces. This task would display the great famine that would overtake the land. Ezekiel also had to take a sharp sword and remove the hair off his face and head, which would show Israel's and Judah's humility as all surrounding nations would witness this great fall of Jerusalem.

Even though Ezekiel gave God the name Jehovah Shammah's to remind Israel of God's restoration of Jerusalem, it is also a testament that God will be present with us during our assignments. As previously discussed, Ezekiel had a great task to accomplish for God. The unusual responsibility that God gave Ezekiel would require unnatural strength from a higher source. This is probably why Ezekiel's name means "God Strengthens." It would seem physically impossible to accomplish all the tasks God placed on Ezekiel. However, God had equipped him for his divine purpose as God will also be there with us during our specific tasks.

Acquiring an assignment from God often means that our adversary is devising his plan. However, God will lift a standard as He is *Jehovah Sabaoth*, the Lord of Host[29]. Receiving a great assignment from God always comes with a battle; however, our God is mighty, having many angels ready for war. Just as King Aram sent an entire army to siege Elisha, our enemy will send his army to attack God's plan. During these moments, we may become dismayed as it seems like we are losing the battle. However, God does not sit on the sidelines during combat. He is our captain, preparing

---

28. Khokhar, "Names for God," line 12.
29. Khokhar, "Names for God," line 11.

an army to fight on our behalf. When Elisha saw Aram's army, he was not afraid as God also sent his host to fight for him. When God gives us an assignment, Satan will send his troops to place barricades around our specific task. However, Elisha told his servant to open his eyes to see God's invisible army that stood before them (2 Kgs 6:8–14).

Each task we receive from God must come with the preparation of war. Every assignment from him means the elevation of his people, and our adversary will not simply lie down while we perform our God-given duty. He sits devising war plans, ready for attack. However, we should understand that God has already decreed and declared our victory. All we must do is open our eyes and see that God has an army ready, willing, and capable of fighting on our behalf. We are never alone in the battle as God shields, protects, and covers us with his grace and mercy. Often, we may not even have to fight in the war because God sends his host to fight before we even arrive.

When the Moabites, Ammonites, and the Meunites came against Judah, King Jehoshaphat began to become discouraged, knowing that his armies could not win against these men. However, the Spirit of the Lord came upon Jahaziel, letting all Judah know that the battle was not theirs, but the Lord's. Their instructions were clear, as King Jehoshaphat was to send those that were conditioned to praise God first in battle. As the men marched into combat, they began singing and praising the God of their salvation, knowing that he had already claimed their victory. Judah did not have to draw one sword as God sent an ambush against the men causing them to fight among themselves (2 Chr 20). When conflicts arise in our lives, send praises first and watch God's host fight and claim the victory.

During the battle, God is *Jehovah Nissi*; the Lord is our banner[30]. We often sing songs and praise God as Jehovah Nissi; however, we may not fully understand this title. The word banner has several definitions. The first one means "a piece of cloth," and the next indicates a "flag or ensign." In this context of the first definition, the Lord is our banner could mean, as Christians, we are clothed with God's righteousness and show forth our victory through him. Ephesians 6:11 admonishes us to "put on the whole armor of God, that we may be able to stand against the wiles of the devil." When we are clothed with the peace and salvation of God, we are preparing ourselves for battle as "we wrestle not against flesh and blood, but against principalities, against powers, against the rulers of darkness of this world,

---

30. "Beautiful Names," line 59.

and against spiritual wickedness in high places" (verse 12). Every day we must clothe our hearts and minds for spiritual warfare. In God's army, we must wear truth, righteousness, peace, faith, salvation, and the Holy Spirit to be prepared for battle.

Several years ago, armies would use war flags to distinguish themselves against their enemies. These flags waved in battle as a tribute to their nation, and many would sacrifice their lives to defend this simple piece of cloth. However, the flag was more than a piece of fabric; but it represented their beliefs and gave them a reason to fight. As Christians, we have fully enlisted in God's army. Jehovah Nissi is a banner that we can hold high to distinguish our faith in him. In this battle, we may be faced with doubt, fear, and disappointments; however, Deuteronomy 20:4 states that God goes into battle for us and fights for our salvation. This is a guaranteed victory, for when we fight, we win.

God had given Gideon that same reassurance over the Midianites. However, Gideon was a simple farmer who felt ill-equipped to lead the Israelites to victory. Over the years, the Midianites grew and caused God's people much trouble. Yet, God had a solution for his people through Gideon. God told him, "Surely, I will be with thee, and thou shalt smite the Midianites as one man" (Judg 6:16). Despite the doubt that Gideon had in his capabilities, he trusted God. Regardless of the troubles that we may face, we must put our trust in God. For this cause, Gideon called God, *Jehovah Shalom*, the Lord our Peace.[31]

During life's trials, we should look to God for our peace. God promises in Isaiah 26:3 that He would keep our minds in perfect harmony as long as we focus on him. Focusing on God means that we must look to him during life's heartaches, failures, and challenges. Our Lord never said that life would be easy, but he did reassure our peace (John 16:33). For the Son of God, who is the Prince of Peace, gave us peace as long as we believe in him (John 14:27). It is not as this world understands it, but it is God-ordained. It shields us from fear and doubt, even when we should be afraid. Knowing that God is for us gives us peace of mind. To have this peace, we must trust in God wholeheartedly, especially when faced with despair. God still reigns supreme overall. The problems that we face are not exempted from God's power. The Word tells us to cast our concerns on him as nothing is too hard for our God (Ps 46:1).

---

31. "Jehovah's Names," lines 36.

Abram was faced with many problems when he learned that Kedorlaomer, the king of Elam, captured his nephew Lot during the Nine Kings War. Abram decided to save Lot despite possible feelings of past deceit from him. Not only this, but he had to choose to get involved in a war that involved many nations. This choice had to be difficult as nine kings were involved in this war. Abram was not a king nor a political figure. He was merely a wealthy man, with many servants. However, despite these significant decisions, Abram gathered 318 trained servants to rescue Lot and other captives.

After the victory, King Melchizedek blessed Abram and praised *Jehovah Eylon*, the Most High God[32], for his triumph against four kings. What was amazing about this encounter was that King Melchizedek was not a Jew but a foreigner who worshiped God as the Israelites. Most non-Israelites worshipped pagan gods. However, this King of Salem recognized Abram's God as the true and living God. He did not hesitate to give God credit for Abram's victory. King Melchizedek understood that the Most High God could do what five kings could not. This one chance meeting allowed Abraham to understand God's power within the world. God pursues people not because of their heritage but because of their hearts. He calls all people, regardless of their background to repentance, and accepts those who are willing to follow and serve him.

When we commit to follow God, he will lead us into a path of righteousness. Therefore, He is called *Jehovah Tsidkenu*; the Lord is Righteous[33] and *Jehovah Tsidkeenu*, The Lord our Righteousness[34]. Often, we talk about righteousness, and we may define it as doing what is right. Yet, other definitions are "being morally good: following religious or moral laws" or "believing something is morally right or fair.[35]" However, a more in-depth look at God's righteousness reveals "the perfection or holiness of his nature.[36]"

The righteousness of God is one of his most essential characteristics. We previously discussed that God is holy, which meant that he dedicates himself to us daily. However, in this text, we can proclaim that God's righteousness is the perfect dedication to those that believe in him. The righteousness of God encompasses many attributes within itself. It means that

---

32. "Jehovah's Names," lines 10.
33. "Jehovah's Names," lines 38.
34. Khokhar, "Names for God," line 9.
35. "Righteousness," lines 1–9.
36. Williams, "Righteousness", lines 33–34.

God judges us honestly as well as God's standards are right and ethical. The declaration that God is righteous means that God's way and deeds are always right, withstanding evil but pursuing what is excellent and correct.

When God's righteousness is revealed, his will for us is also uncovered. One of the most righteous acts that God performed was sacrificing his Son on the cross for our sins. Second Corinthians 5:21 states, "He made Him who knew no sin to be sin on our behalf so that we might become the righteousness of God in Him." Undisputedly, a debt had to be paid for our sins. Romans 6:23 tells us that the wages of sin are death. Consequently, therefore in the Old Testament, pure animals without blemish had to be sacrificed. However, God realized that this payment could not be fulfilled by goats, bullocks, or lambs but through a divine atonement. For us to become the sons and daughters of God, it was clear that Jesus had to be the ultimate sacrifice. This is a testament to God's righteousness. Despite Jesus' pureness from sin, God's moral conduct would not allow sin to go uncovered. Therefore, his only begotten Son had to die.

God's name Yahweh and Jehovah, proves that God is genuinely I AM, meaning that He is everything we need him to be. We have learned that this God-given name encompasses many different attributes of our Creator. Through his name, "I AM," we understand him to be absolute in all his power and His ways. The primary notion of this name is that God is Lord. God as Lord means that our God rules over everything. Even though God is the definitive ruler, some do not allow his power to reign supreme in their lives. It is crucial that, as believers, we recognize Jehovah as the highest authority overall. When we call God our Lord, it is merely not a label, but it is a confession that our lives are not our own, but they belong to the Lord, who is Jehovah.

Chapter 4

GOD, THE FATHER

"And, I will be a Father to you, and you will be my sons and daughters, says the Lord Almighty"

2 CORINTHIANS 6:18, NIV

OUR SOCIETY PLACES MUCH importance on the father or father figure. Despite cultural diversity, it appears that the role of the father is parallel across the board. Traditionally, fathers have been protectors and providers for their offspring. Causing children raised in fatherless homes to be significantly disadvantaged as fathers impact their overall development. Children without father figures often battle low self-esteem, behavioral problems, sexual promiscuity, and juvenile delinquency[1]. Moreover, they seem to have a reduced sense of self due to the missing link in their heredity. Fortunately, we have a spiritual Father who is an excellent substitute for those lacking their natural ones.

The Bible tells fathers to "train up a child in the way he should go, and when he is old, he will not depart from it" (Prov 22:6). Fathers are often seen as the household's disciplinarians, providing rules and expecting their children to abide by those guidelines. Likewise, God, our Father, provides instructions on how we should live. He gave us the commandments, which mainly tells us how to honor him and humanity (Exod 20:12–17). He told

---

1. Meyers, "Fatherless Daughters," 3–88.

us to love one another (John 13:34-35; I John 5:3) and have faith in him (Heb 11:6). Most of all, our Father requires that we be just, love mercy, and walk humbly in him (Mic 6:8). Following these guidelines demonstrates that we are his children. Likewise, not keeping them makes us bastards and not sons (Heb 12:8).

Being an illegitimate child means that their parents conceived the child out of wedlock[2]. However, this may pose the question, how can we be illegitimate if God is not married? As a husband and wife are one, we are joined together with God by his spirit (1 Cor 6:17). In Jeremiah 3:14, the Lord says that he is married to the backslider. God demonstrates the union that he has with his children as his Son unites us all. The Bible speaks of this union as we are created in Christ (Eph 2:10), crucified with him (Gal 2:20), and united with him in death as well as the resurrection (Rom 6:5). Therefore, those who are not joined with Christ are not associated with him. Ungodly is their way as they live in the flesh, not resembling the Father's character. Each person has the right to become a child of God; however, we must receive him as our Father (John 1:12-13). Consequently, those who do not recognize God as Father destroy the union, ultimately divorcing God, causing them to become illegitimate children.

Genetic makeup allows children to have similar characteristics to their biological fathers. We are all made in the likeness of God; however, all humans do not take on his full image. As his children, it is befitting for us to possess the same qualities as our heavenly Father. Similarly, our spiritual DNA will cause us to resemble God. Galatians 5:22-23 speaks of the qualities we should own, given that we are God's children. Meditating and walking in the Spirit allows us to have a mindset concerning our heavenly Father. Likewise, those who walk in the flesh will live accordingly, having a hostile mind towards him (Rom 8:5-7). On one occasion, Jesus said, "ye are of your father, the devil, and the lusts of your father ye will do" (John 8:44). Concisely, those who do not resemble God look a lot like their father, Satan.

Being in God's image is not merely a physical attribute, but spiritual as we are his perfect workmanship (Eph 2:10). Realistically, we look at our natural state, and self-doubt seems to get the best of us. However, God has equipped us with every spiritual blessing when He adopted us as sons and daughters through his Son, Jesus Christ (Eph 1:3-6). Thankfully, God's adoption is not like the world's. There is no waiting period, no paperwork, no costly fees. His adoption comes with immediate entrance into his family

---

2. "Illegitimate," lines 1-2.

as we become newly restored in him. Similarly, we are blessed with his grace, freed from sin, and have access to his divine wisdom. Due to this, our dispositions, behaviors, and actions begin to represent our heavenly Father. If our characteristics and activities do not match God's, we may need a spiritual paternity test to determine who truly is our father.

Unquestionably, children who have little knowledge of their father are ill-equipped to connect to who they are as individuals. Self-understanding is a vital key to a person's growth, whether it be natural or spiritual. Naturally, a child with limited information about their father may have a lack of self-identification. Our development, whether it is physiological or social, begins with our parents. Biologically speaking, parents give a child's genes, which ultimately determines their physical characteristics. A child's temperament is also a trait that comes from their mothers and fathers. Children who only know one parent are at a disadvantage as they are missing a vital piece of their identity.

This occurrence often happens in the church as individuals claim to know God as their Father. However, they do not know who they are in him. To know God is one of the first steps in distinguishing who we are as his children. We have declared God as King of Kings and Lord of Lords, wherefore if we are his children, then we are adopted into a royal priesthood, chosen by him to be holy because he is holy (1 Pet 2:9). Often, we quote this Scripture, however, do we earnestly believe it. God predestined us to be related to him as sons and daughters, through his Son (Gal 3:26). This is a glorious revelation that God has chosen us. Yet, our inadequate self-image blinds who we are in him. Despite being God's perfect masterpiece, we still find ourselves feeling impoverished, defeated, and insignificant. Somehow our self-concept becomes clouded, and we began to lose sight of our royal status.

First, John 3:2 states, "Beloved, now we are the sons of God, and it doth not yet appear what we shall be: but we know that, when he shall appear, we shall be like him; for we shall see him as he is." Despite our current state, we will be fully changed when the Son of God comes. In this life, our society puts a lot of stock in physical appearance, wealth, and status. However, God has given us a magnificent promise that we will be like his beloved Son, Jesus Christ. He is the all-knowing Father, who formed us before the world's foundation and knew his final plan for us. How we are now merely is irrelevant to how we will be.

He has made us kings and priests through his divine blood to reign with him forever (Rev 1:6). We are a part of the royal family; we shall receive crowns of glory and righteousness (1 Pet 5:4). God will reward our faithfulness with authorities over cities and land (Luke 19:17), and we shall inherit the earth and all that is in it (Matt 5:5). Regardless of how we view ourselves today, our outlook is far greater than we can expect.

Although we know the wonderful things God has in store for us, we still crave tangibility in this lifetime. Even though we are not living in mansions and have celebrity status, God still sees value in us. None of God's children are insignificant in his eyes as he has given us diverse spiritual gifts to fulfill the great commission. In First Corinthians 12, Paul determines that we are the body of Christ working in different arenas towards the same goal. In our natural bodies, each of our internal and external parts works together, forming a figure that is capable of existing. When one of those parts malfunctions, it does not mean that the body must succumb to death, but it means that the other parts must work that much harder to survive.

Subsequently, this is the same notion that Apostle Paul discussed concerning the church of God. Each of us is valuable to our Father's kingdom and carries a specific task that needs to be accomplished. If one member is not there, it doesn't mean the church stops functioning. However, the other members must compensate for that loss. If the usher is not at their post, then perhaps the church custodian must greet parishioners instead of ensuring the sanctuary's cleanliness. If the musician is not present, the congregation must fight a little harder in praise and worship. These positions may seem minor compared to church leaders; however, they are crucial for the church's proper execution.

Impairments tend to develop when members discount their ability to add to the body of Christ. Unfortunately, there are many disabled churches unable to operate in God due to full dismemberment. Centuries ago, dismemberment was a form of capital punishment used to pull or cut the limbs off the body. Ironically, this is still occurring in today's churches, unknowingly allowing for the disfigurement of the body of Christ. Naively, churches are being destroyed as members or cut down and pulled apart, often not by our adversary but by each other. Idly we sit paralyzed, powerless to move. We are physically destroyed because we are spiritually incapacitated.

Within our human bodies, each member works collectively to ensure that the body continues to function appropriately as it should in the body of Christ. Christ is the head of the church (Eph 5:23). The head functions as a regulator of all that occur within the body, ultimately directing the different members. Pastors support Christ as the neck supports the weight of the head. In our human bodies, the neck transmits information from the head to the rest of the body. Spiritually, pastors distinctively hear from God, and their job is to communicate the message He has given to the rest of the church body. Another characteristic of the neck is that it is "flexible allowing the head to turn and flex in all directions." As the neck is flexible, allowing the head to move in different directions, pastors need to be accommodating to the move of Christ within their churches.

Ironically, the neck cannot move opposite of the head. Wherever the head moves, the neck must follow. Therefore, this is how it should be with Christ and the angel of the church. When Christ shifts, so does the pastor. Within the natural, we can experience neck cramps when both go in opposing directions. Unfortunately, our churches cannot afford a spiritual neck spasm. When this happens naturally, we are forced to turn our entire bodies to allow the head to move. Similarly, within the spirit, if the pastors don't obey, our heavenly Father will move the whole church body until the pastor spasms stops.

Another body part is the shoulder as it stabilizes the neck. Often it "bears a heavy load[3]" because it is the most movable joint within the body, having the most significant "range of motion." Deacons are considered the church's shoulders, bearing the pastor's weight to do their spiritual duties. Leading the body of Christ is a difficult task, and it becomes even more challenging with weak shoulders. Pastors need strong deacons. Noted the shoulders are the most movable joint within the body, and the deacon's primary role is to move in the direction in which the church needs them to move, whether it is logistical or spiritual.

Within the human body, the torso is made up of many organs crucial to the bodies functioning. The torso's job is to protect the body's weaker internal members, such as the heart, lungs, and kidneys[4]. These organs are vital to living, and if they are unprotected, then the body dies. Ministers of the gospel are considered the torso of the body of Christ. Their job is to protect the members from the enemy that tries to "kill, steal, and destroy them" through the Word of God.

3. Jain, "Preventing," lines 1.
4. "Torso," lines 2- 4.

Lastly, the appendages, which include our legs and arms, are elements of the body that are "attached to something larger." These body parts can be considered the church congregation. Often people discount being a church member because there isn't a specific title. However, without an assembly, there wouldn't be anyone to take hold of the Word of God. Some ministers have said, "they will preach to the pews." Maybe they have forgotten that the pews are without souls and cannot enter the Kingdom of Heaven. Also, the pews are stationary and are not equipped to spread the gospel. At the very least, they can't pay tithes or give offerings to improve the church. Preaching to an empty church profits nothing, but having members, whether it is a few or many, is gain. Therefore, our job isn't limited to just warming a church pew, yet we should dedicate ourselves to God through hearing and fellowshipping with one another (Acts 2:42). Our natural hands grasp objects as our legs are made to stand as well as move. Within the body of Christ, the members are likened to the hands and the legs that can hold fast to the gospel, stand on God's word, walk in the Spirit, and run swiftly, spreading the good news of Jesus Christ.

The improvement of the Kingdom depends on our diverse positions within the body of Christ. Even though siblings are raised within the same household, they still have unique roles. This is the same notion for the church of God as He has given us individuals within the ministry (Eph 4:11). A calling within the five-fold ministry is valid and essential "for the perfecting of the saints"; however, we should not feel neglected if we are exempted from these titles. Yet, we should rejoice in the spiritual gifts our Father has given.

No grateful child rejects a gift from their father unless they are willing to suffer the consequences. However, within the body of Christ, we allow our skills to remain idle, tending to become upset with the consequential impact. In Matthew 25:14–30, Jesus spoke of the outcomes for those who sit uselessly. Within this parable, we find two types of Christians, those willing to use their abilities and those who are unmindful of the importance of their gift. No matter what a person's talents may be, they are from the Lord (1 Cor 12: 4–6). Each of us has exceptional aptitudes within the spirit and the natural that can be utilized within the church. Whether our gift is prophecy or parking cars, we must do it to the glory of our Father. Regardless of our specific task, we should never neglect it as it is a God-assigned gift (1 Tim 4:14).

God, The Father

Everyone will not be a part of the five-fold ministry; however, God requires workers behind the scenes: supporting cast ministries. Serving in these roles may come with little recognition as the congregation may not flock to see Sister Margaret clean the church or Deacon Earnest turn on the heat. However, these tasks are essential. On any given Sunday, if they forget to do their job, the members will take notice. Their role may seem insignificant because they are not at the forefront, they are still vital to the ministry. Despite the position that we play, we should sincerely perfect it as we do it not unto others, but God (Col 3:23).

Perfecting our talents within the body of Christ will bring forth our rewarded inheritance (Col 3:24). Proverbs 13:22 states, "A good man leaves an inheritance to his children's children (NKJV). Naturally, most good fathers want to leave a legacy for their children and, in some cases, for their grandchildren. This is the blueprint that God has given as he promises a divine inheritance for his children. We are heirs of the Father and joint-heirs of his Son (Rom 8:17). Whatever belongs to Jesus will also belong to the Father's sons and daughters. However, to gain this inheritance, we must continue the work that Jesus did and perfect our spiritual gifts to do more outstanding works for the Kingdom of our Father (John 14:12-14).

It does not profit Christians to be lazy or slothful in fulfilling the great commission as often our labor and commitment to God may bring forth heartache and suffering. However, Timothy believed that we should endure hardship like a good soldier (2 Tim 2:3). Before soldiers go into battle, they experience basic training to learn how to defend and serve their country. Being a good soldier means that we are alert, aware, and attentive to the enemy's attacks. However, we cannot become effective soldiers if we do not experience our spiritual boot camp. Challenging as it may be, God's training will produce well-prepared men and women equipped to serve and protect. The preparation may be complicated; however, we must rest assured that our General is mighty in battle, and He has never lost a fight.

Being in our Father's army does not release us from persecution, yet there is comfort within godly suffering. We may feel that we are losing the battle, but we will not lose the war. As children of God, we must understand that our current suffering will not compare to the glory revealed in us (Rom 8:18). However, it is merely testing our faith. No battle is won by giving up, but we must endure until the end (Matt 10:22). Endurance kept Jesus on the cross, and this same strength is within us. Being a good soldier can be difficult, but when our faith is tried, we know that we will gain greater confidence in God.

Demonstrating our faith in God allows him to be our paternal protector, provider, and disciplinarian. Characteristically, these are the primary roles of the head of the household. The father seems to be the first line of defense in protecting the family, which is the same concept in God. Our Father fights for us, and no weapon that is formed against us shall prosper (Isa 54:17). Most children have experienced some form of bullying and will quickly run to their fathers for safety. As children of God, we are not exempted from spiritual bullying as our adversary strategizes to intimidate (John 10:10). However, when the enemy comes in like a flood, our Father prepares for battle, putting on the breastplate of righteousness, a helmet of salvation, clothing himself with vengeance, to fight for his children (Isa 59:17-19).

Just as a natural father provides for his family, our holy Father makes provisions for us. No good father denies their children of basic needs, and if we are less than God, then how much more will our spiritual Father provide for us (Matt 7:11). Unconsciously, we place limits on God as we tend to only think of him supplying necessary resources. However, there are no parameters in his divine provisions. He offers healing for the sick (Ps 41:3), peace of mind for the wearied (Matt 11:28-29), redemption for the sinner (Isa 44:22), strength to the weak (2 Cor 12:9-10), power to the powerless (Col 1:29) deliverance to the captive (Nah 1:13), and victory to the defeated (I Corinthian 15:57). Most of all, when we come short of his glory, he is rich in mercy (Eph 2:4).

Even though God's mercy and compassion flow to all his creation (Ps 145:9), our Father is a disciplinarian when we are disobedient. Parents use methods of discipline to correct unwanted behavior. Proverbs 13:24 states, "Whoever spares the rod hates their children, but the one who loves their children is careful to discipline them (NIV). The love of God will not allow his children to be overtaken by sin, yet He chastises us to correct our undesirable behaviors. God wants us to share in his holiness as sons and daughters, and He deals with us accordingly. As we become adults, we recognize our youthful mistakes and respect our father's correction. Therefore, we should rejoice in the fact that our heavenly Father loves us enough to discipline us for our good (Heb 12:9).

Unfortunately, as children grow older, they forget the teachings and guidance of their parents. Most teens are eager to reach adulthood as our federal government gives them legal privileges and responsibilities. Regrettably, most of their choices result in negative consequences. These choices were indeed demonstrated within the parable of the prodigal son (Luke 15:11–32). Undoubtedly, the son wanted a life outside his father's rules. However, in the end, he learned the dire costs of his poor decision-making.

Most Christians are like the prodigal son, wanting the Father's blessings but not wanting to abide by his guidelines. Instead, we waste our divine inheritance on earthly pleasures versus thinking about our wondrous blessings in Heaven. Surrendering to God's will is more comfortable than the aftermath of living without him. Existing without God is reckless as our sole survival depends upon him. There are only two wills: the will of God or the will of the flesh. Ignoring God's will leads to a path of destruction. However, choosing to surrender redeems us to our rightful place with the Father.

Just like the father in the parable, our heavenly Father welcomes us with open arms. He doesn't boast in being right or bellows a melody of "I told you so's"; however, He invites us to communion and rests in him. Despite our rebellion, He doesn't handle us as servants, but He treats us as sons. When one of God's children returns, the angels celebrate and rejoice in Heaven (Luke 15:10). Just the same, the prodigal son's father delighted in his arrival, saying, "For this my son was dead, and is alive again; he was lost, and is found" (Luke 15:24 ESV). Undisputedly, this is probably what our heavenly Father says when we decide to come back home.

Like an eager parent awaits their child's homecoming, our heavenly Father waits for us. God desires that we inherit the Kingdom of Heaven as this was the plan since the world's foundation (Matt 25:34). In the natural, when children return home, the parents often spruce up their child's bedroom in preparation for their arrival. Can we imagine the Son of God, anticipating our arrival, preparing our mansion for us (John 14:2)? The concept of Jesus preparing a mansion is challenging when God's throne is heaven and his footstool is the earth (Isa 66:1). If heaven is a chair and the world is a place God rests his feet, then how significant will our inheritance be? "No eye has seen, no ear has heard, and no mind has imagined what God has prepared for those who love him" (1 Cor 2:9 NIV).

Loving God brings forth significant advantages, and since our Father has shown unconditional love for us, we, in turn, choose to fear him (I John 4:19). Loving and fearing God may seem contradictory. However, the fear of the Lord is paralleled to loving him. Fear in this context means that we stand in awe of his power, strength, and love. We understand the magnitude of God's love as He gave his only begotten Son for ransom for us. However, for those who love him in return, he will prolong their life (Prov 10:27), protect them from evil (Prov 19:23), give them riches and honor (Prov 22:4), provide them mercy (Luke 1:50), and give them his unwavering favor (Ps 147:11).

Developing love for God does not happen in one occurrence; however, it must mature over time. As Christians, we should not discount this process; our love for God should continually increase. We should love God with our whole heart, soul, strength, and mind, meaning we ought to dedicate our lives to understanding his ways and stature (Luke 10:27). Our devotion towards him does not increase with avoidance or distance. However, falling in love with God comes by pursuing him through open communication, studying his Word, and abiding by it. It's impossible to say we love God if we do not know him. Knowing him creates vulnerability within ourselves to expose every hidden weakness and allow the Father's love to provide a covering over them.

Psalm 9:10 says, "they that know thy name will put their trust in thee: for thou, Lord, hast not forsaken them that seek thee." When we develop closeness with God, we are indeed able to call him by the name Father. Often, some Christians have even called God "daddy" to show their intimate relationship with him. Calling God these "pet names" or terms of endearment derives from the close relationship that progresses over time. Within the new testament, Jesus and Apostle Paul had a strong connection with God because they trusted him. Through that relationship, they began to call God *Abba*, which originated from a Semitic language, meaning father[5].

Little is known about Paul's biological father. However, sources state that He was a Pharisees. These people often did not agree with Jesus's interpretation of the Law, which caused him to expose their self-righteousness and hypocrisy (Matt 23:13–39; Luke 11:42). Paul's learning about the law had to come from his natural father. However, once Paul met Jesus, he denounced his father's teachings to become an adopted son of God. A further assumption could be that his father also disassociated himself from him. After all, Paul was now an enemy and preached against everything he previously learned as a child. Consequently, Paul's devotion to God was an actual adoption as he had lost his natural father.

---

5. "Abba," lines 1–2.

God, The Father

Within the Bible, there are two occurrences in which Apostle Paul called God Abba (Rom 8:15 and Gal 4:6). On both occasions, Paul was speaking to Gentiles in Corinth and Galatia. During this time, salvation was only for the Jews, as they were God's chosen people (Deut 7:6). Making good on his conversion, Paul vigorously preached Christ to the Gentiles. Israel was God's chosen people and had a special covenant with him. Historically, the Gentiles were thought to be outsiders worshipping pagan gods. Even at the beginning of Jesus's ministry, he instructed the disciples to preach only to the Jews (Matt 10:5–15). Even though Paul was of Jewish descent, he could relate to the Gentiles, as they both felt unworthy to be accepted by God. By calling God Abba, Paul showed his undying love to a Father who he once rejected but never rejected him.

Before his transformation, Paul was a prosecutor of Christian followers. Previously being a Pharisees, Paul opposed the fact that Jesus was indeed the Messiah, and often the Pharisees criticized Jesus along with his disciples for not observing the Mosaic Law. Specifically, the Bible does not mention the prosecution that Christians endured under Paul. However, in detail, Paul described the cruelty he encountered as a follower of Christ (2 Cor11:13–24). Assumingly, this is perhaps the same torture Paul rendered to Christian believers. If that is the case, then in no reasonable way would God adopt a man who victimized those who believed in his Son, Jesus Christ.

Adoption into the royal family was implausible for a man like Paul. Past faults should have confiscated his right to be even associated with God, let alone called his son. However, Paul recognized that his past could not interfere with his future (Phil3:13–14). As believers, we should adopt this same mindset. Frequently, we allow our past lives to overshadow the adoption that God has granted to us. Despite Paul's past failings, he decided to "press towards the mark." Regardless of our past deeds, the Father's love remembers them no more. Who we were does not compare to who we are currently in him.

At the garden of Gethsemane, Jesus also referred to God as Abba during his infamous prayer (Mark 14:36). This cry was likened to a child's whimper for his parents, especially when they are crying for help, begging, or scared. Children will call for their parents, using pet names, calling out each syllable, making the "mommy" or "daddy" last longer than it should. This almost unbearable screeching sound alarms the parent that their child needs them. In this reference, Jesus was the begging child. Knowing full well the agony and pain he would face, he pleaded with his Father, beckoning for "Abba to remove the cup." Abba was Jesus' cry for help. Not just for that night, but from the last events that led to it.

While in Bethany, a woman with an alabaster box prepared Jesus' living body for death. Ceremonially, people only did this after the person died, but Jesus underwent this death ritual while still alive. Symbolically, this is likened to the coroner placing a toe tag on a person who is still physically walking. Or the undertaker preparing a grave while the person is still alive. Envision how grief-stricken our Lord had to be, knowing this oil was anointing his body for death. Imagine the sorrow he must felt when his disciples tried to stop the ceremonious act.

Jesus called for Abba, as perhaps this was the first sign of abandonment as his disciples appeared to care more about the financial gain versus the spiritual. Undoubtedly, their intentions were good; however, there was a greater need they were unable to see. Preparing his body for death was more important than providing for the poor. The disciples were merely concerned about a temporary problem, while Jesus' death would be the ultimate solution to every predicament. Planning for his death was also forecasting our victory in his rising. Yet Jesus' disciples attempted to stop this act by being less concerned about our Lord and more concerned about their problems.

It was not enough that Jesus had to carry the weight of death and sin as well as the feeling of disloyalty. Jesus cried for Abba as the twelve disciples who had once followed him would soon scatter at even the mention of his name. One would betray him, the other would deny him, and Jesus was ultimately alone. No one came to his trial, and there were no pleads of his innocence, no fancy lawyer, no character witnesses. Discarded like a thief, Jesus found himself alone at his lowest state.

"Pray with me for one hour."

For three years, Jesus equipped and mentored these twelve men. He provided teachings about God, told them how to pray, and prepared them to follow in his footsteps. For three years, one thousand and ninety-five days, the Lord met their personal and spiritual needs, asking nothing in return. However, when Gethsemane became Jesus' personal death row, they were found fast asleep.

"Pray with me for one hour."

It was a simple request that fell short of its appeal. When Jesus needed them, they were unable to answer the call. Not only did he feel abandoned by his friends, but he felt neglected by his Father. At Calvary, Jesus cried, "Eli, Eli, lema sabachthani? My God, my God, why hast thou forsaken me?" Notice, Jesus stated God versus Abba. The connection between son and father had been separated by sin. As his Son hung defiled on the cross, God's back was turned, his ears plugged, and his eyes closed. For eternity Jesus was in the presence of his Father. Even throughout his human life, God was still there from conception until the cross. He was there in the garden of Gethsemane, there when he was arrested; there when he was on trial. However, from the moment he was connected to the cross, the Father and Son's connection was contaminated by sin.

Specifically, we do not know how many hours Jesus hung on the cross as we estimate at least six hours (John 19:14). However, the Son of God did not want to be without his Father for even one minute. Imagine if we had this same passion for God if we desired to be with the Father every waking moment of our lives. Considerably Jesus understood that his Father did not forsake him. However, it was the awful stench of sin he wore for us. For those few hours, the eternal relationship between Jesus and the Father had stopped, and he felt the unbearable pain of being alone. This agonizing feeling of abandonment had to occur so Jesus could relate to our feelings of desertion by God.

Often, we feel abandoned by our Father. However, He never leaves us. We tend to reject him. Unfortunately, it is the stench of sin that separates us from him. Thankfully, Jesus understands this separation and becomes an unfailing intercessor who pleads our case. As it was recorded in Isaiah, our iniquities separate us from God; sin and God cannot coexist (59:2). They are two unmixable elements; like oil and water, they cannot commingle. Therefore, salvation comes by Jesus, who appeals to his Father for all humankind. As a criminal defense attorney, the Son of God sits on his father's right hand, pleading our case before the highest judge. By his intercessions, we can reconcile the relationship between ourselves and the eternal Father. Even though we are guilty of sin, God finds us innocent, and perhaps this is why Apostle Paul called God *the Father of Mercies* (2 Cor 1:3).

Indeed, Paul could testify to God's everlasting compassion towards him. Even though God forgave Paul, it seems he did not get by squeaky clean for his prior acts. Suffering was a part of his ministry, and only through God's grace was he able to sustain the numerous trials and tribulations he faced (Acts 9:16). While in Asia, Paul's life was threatened (Acts 17: 5–7), he was arrested and imprisoned (Acts 22:24), shipwrecked in Malta (Acts

27:41 to 28:1), beaten with rods (Acts 16:23), and stoned facing death in Lystra (Acts 14:19). Not only this, but forty men vowed not to eat or drink anything until they killed him (Acts 23:12–35). However, through all this, Paul still saw God's continuing kindness that was given to him.

Unquestionably, Paul appeared to suffer more than any other apostle of the New Testament. On one occasion, he revealed having a "thorn in his flesh." There is no indication of what this "thorn" had been. However, Paul was so desperate to have it removed he sought the Lord three times. Whether it was a physical ailment, emotional distress, persecutors, or a combination of these things, God was still able to deliver Paul from it. Nevertheless, God stated, "His grace was sufficient, and His strength would be made perfect in his weakness (2 Cor 12:9). The "thorn" could have easily hindered Paul; however, God's mercy kept him throughout his ministry.

As believers, we often ask God to free us from life's challenges. He is the Almighty God; nothing is impossible for him, right? Of course, God could efficiently deliver us from life's "thorns." However, which one is more impressive: God removing the obstacle or God giving us the strength to go through the problem? God's grace is enough. There are no problems that can overtake believers if God abounds in mercy. Since his mercy endures forever, there is absolutely nothing that can destroy God's unmerited favor in our lives. In one of Paul's messages, he stated, "we are troubled on every side, yet not distressed; we are perplexed, but not in despair, persecuted, but not forsaken; cast down, but not destroyed" (2 Cor 4:7–8). Indeed, we will have shortcomings, heartaches, disappointments, and regrets in this life, yet through all this, God's mercy keeps us from falling.

Along with God's mercy, the light of God keeps us from the darkness. Due to this, James called God the *Father of Lights* (Jas1:7). Theologians have debated on whether James was referring to the children of God or the lights in the sky. God, the Father as well as the Son, are both referenced as being light. In I John 1:5 it states, "God is light," and in John 8:12, Jesus says, "I am the light of the world." Therefore, if our heavenly Father is light, and Jesus is light, then we as his children are also light.

Resembling the light of God means that we accept these characteristics within ourselves. Light is "a natural agent that stimulates sight and makes things visible." The noun sense of this word is also descriptive of God. Our spiritual agent arouses divine sight, opening eyes from darkness to light (Acts 26:18). This illuminating light caused Saul to lose his eyesight temporarily, and this same light provided him spiritual vision (Acts

9:3–17). Encountering the light of God should cause believers to become blind to sin, producing an awakening in God. God's eyes are not limited by natural sight, yet his eyes are divine. Identifying with God means that we can see within the spiritual realm. As his children, there is no feasible way we can walk in the spirit if we are spiritually blinded by darkness.

The light of God outshines the gloom of sin. Within the biblical text, darkness often is symbolic of evil deeds. Descriptively speaking, the night is uncertain, cold, and lonely. If a person walks in darkness, they wander, stumbling and tripping over unseen items. Comparatively, this is the case for those who are bound by sin. It causes the children of God to walk towards unclear circumstances, toppling over life's obstacles, and falling into a pit of dismay. Our iniquities handicap us with spiritual blindfolds as we take the hand of Satan, who recklessly guides us to a destructive future. David said the word of God is a lamp unto his feet and a light for his path (Ps 119:105). God's light helps us maneuver around the trap of the enemy, causing us to walk on a divine path of righteousness. It doesn't mean that the children of God will not fall. However, it means His light will help us find a way to get back up (Prov 24:16).

The light of God can also be referenced to the verb tense of light, which means "to start burning or ignite." Being born of the Father means that we have the gift of the Holy Spirit and fire. In examining the abilities of fire, we know that it burns and consumes. These are the same characteristics of the Holy Ghost. It burns out sin and ignites the power within us. On the day of Pentecost, the Holy Spirit came through like a "mighty rushing wind," filling all that were present as they spoke with "tongues of fire" (Acts 2:2–4). Fire catches quickly and is not easily contained; so, it is with the Spirit of God. As children of God, He has given us power and authority to be a light unto the world: to come forth like a violent wind extinguishing every evil device of the enemy.

During the Sermon on the Mount, Jesus said, we are a city of lights that cannot be hidden (Matt 5:14). Henceforth, we are to let our light shine and do the good works of our Father. The light of God cannot be stifled or put out, yet it glistens during darkness. The Lord's radiance is like the sunlight that shines strong in the murkiest weather (Hab 3:4). Miraculously, this same trait was also passed on to his children as we have this same everlasting flame within us. Therefore, our light should shine as brilliant as the sun so that we can lead a clear path to the Son.

As the Father of Lights, God could also be distinguished by the fact that He created the sun, moon, and stars. A good portion of the first chapter of Genesis is dedicated to the formation of these light sources. Even though God gave the sun and the moon ability to rule over day and night, they are still subjected to him. Both elements obey the laws of God. Have we ever considered what would happen if these light sources decided to defy God? What would be the outcome if the sun decided to move 5 percent closer or a few miles away from the earth's atmosphere? The unfortunate answer is that we would cease to exist[6]. Gratefully, these sources of light submit to his law, like all God's creation. It appears that the only part of the creation disobedient to God are the ones He blessed to be in his image.

Hebrews 12:9 warns the children of God to be obedient to the *Father of Spirits*. Today it is not uncommon for fathers to be imprisoned with their sons. The reasoning is because children are impressionable, imitating the actions of their environment. Indeed, we have heard the saying, "you're just like your father." This contemptuous phrase is often said to children who reveal the same undesirable traits as their natural fathers. Repeatedly hearing that phrase creates self-fulling prophecies as the child will gain the same unwelcome characteristics. On the contrary, as children of God, we should do our best to replicate the same qualities as our heavenly father. If we resemble the spirit of God, we can take delight in hearing someone say, "you're just like your Father."

As sons and daughters, we have God's spirit dwelling within us (Rom 8:9): the spirit of wisdom, understanding, counsel, might, knowledge, and fear of the Lord (Isa 11:2–3). Just as blood flows throughout our natural body, the life-producing spirit of God moves within us. God told Ezekiel he would give the children of Israel a new heart and would put his spirit in them to keep his commandments (Ezek 36:26–27). Our natural flesh is made of a sinful nature, willing to disobey the commands of God. However, those born of the spirit die to the flesh, causing total submission to God's will.

Disobedience often leads to calamity, yet the fear of the Lord empowers spiritual obedience. As the first chosen king of Israel, King Saul had many victories. However, his repeated disobedience caused the Father to replace his spirit with an evil nature, ultimately leading to his unfortunate demise (I Sam 16:14). Inversely, when the spirit of the Lord came upon Zechariah (ben Jehoiada), he boldly disclosed the sins of Israel and was

---

6. Opfer, "What if Earth," lines 22–27

immediately stoned to death (2 Chr 24:40). Zechariah could have easily dismissed the Spirit of the Lord and lived; however, it was the fear of God that caused him to react shamelessly against Israel's rebelliousness. Like Zechariah, we must realize that fearing God and dying is better than fearing death and living.

Ironically, the word spirit comes from the Latin word *spiritus*, which means breath[7]. The spirit of God or the breath of God brings forth life. Ezekiel prophesied to the dry bones and the wind, so the breath of God could command them to live. Not only did God call them out of their graves, but he put his spirit inside of them (Ezek 37:1–14). The vision of the dry bones was the vision of the rebirthing of Israel. God's spirit can cause a revival of any dead situations in our lives. If we have the spirit of God dwelling in us, we can speak life to our circumstances, calling them out of their tombs to live.

However, in the same manner, disobeying God could have fatal consequences. Lot's wife made the error of observing Sodom and Gomorrah's city, even after the angels advised against it. There's no explicit reference to why she turned around, just the consequences of her actions. Perhaps she was startled by the raining fire and brimstone, or maybe she worried about the safety of her daughters. Maybe curiosity got the best of her. Or she was overwhelmed with compassion, as the sound of the dying became too much to bear. Whatever the reason, her disobedience was met with a fatal penalty. Often, we tend to criticize Lot's wife. However, are we any better? One glance costed her life. How many times have we sinned against God and were spared? When will our one simple act of disobedience be our last?

Most children know how to test the waters before getting into trouble with their parents. Contemptuously, God's children are no different than the child who sneaks a cookie from the cookie jar or comes home fifteen minutes late after curfew. The reward normally outweighs the punishment, so the child does as they please. Certainly, we do not want to be compared to a disobedient child, but we are the same. As children of God, we tend to ignore the Spirit because we take advantage of his mercy and compassion. God says fast, but perhaps our desire for breakfast outweighed his request. The Father says to pray, yet we instead watch television versus hearkening to the voice of the Lord. He may say read, but we rather sleep. God does not want us to obey the large commands, but he tests us with the small ones as well.

---

7. "Spiritus," line 2.

Pastor Steven Furtick once said, "simple acts of obedience usually precede great moves of God."[8] This was certainly the case for Peter. Despite his knowledge of fishing, Peter's simple act of obedience led to becoming the rock Jesus would build his church (Luke 5:1–7; Matt 16:18). Peter could have easily denied Jesus' request. After all, Peter was a skilled fisherman who understood the science behind fishing. However, he decided to obey Jesus' command. By this one single moment of obedience, Peter's entire world changed. Not only his but the lives of all who would be saved under his ministry.

Christians must be obedient to the spirit of God our Father. What would have happened if Peter allowed his knowledge of fishing to override Jesus' request? Would the lame be able to walk (Acts 3:2–11), would the dead be able to wake (Acts 9:40), would three thousand souls be added to the Kingdom (Acts 2:14–42)? Our obedience is not linked to only our salvation but to those who wait on us. There are people spiritually waiting on our calling within the ministry, but the longer we decide to rebel against God, the longer people are waiting on deliverance. Each one of God's children has a divine assignment. Like Peter, what will our one act of obedience lead to in our walk-in Christ?

As Christians, we should be filled with the spirit of knowledge and wisdom to make reasonable but Godly decisions. "There is a way that seems right to a man, but its end is the way of death" (Prov 14:12). Likewise, we should never lean to our understanding but seek counsel from God (Prov 3:5–6). Apostle Paul believed that our mindset should be like the Son of God, who gave his life through obedience versus being dissenting to his Father's will (Phil2:5–11). Therefore, Apostle Paul prayed, "That the God of our Lord Jesus Christ, the Father of glory, may give unto you the spirit of wisdom and revelation in knowledge of him" (Eph 1:17).

The knowledge of God keeps us in his glory. As previously distinguished, God's glory represents the splendor of his majestic power in all the earth. The entire globe is filled with it as "the earth is the Lord's and the fullness thereof, the world, and all that dwells in it (Ps 24:1). The power of God abides in the earth as no one can raise the sun, control the winds, and command the rain. This authority belongs to God alone. He is the mighty King of Glory that rules over every living creature as there is no one stronger than him (Ps 24:7–10). However, when Paul called God, The *Father of*

---

8. Furtick, "The Pastor's Workshop," 1

Glory, this did not only recognize him as having complete control, yet it signified him as the *creator* of power, might, and strength.

In the natural, a woman's egg lies dormant within her body until the male fertilizes it with his seed. Without this process, there is no life. The unfertilized egg is inactive, without purpose, so it is released from the woman's body. As the father provides life through conception, God is the creator of spiritual life, and without him, we spiritually do not exist. Seemingly, a woman does not name her unused eggs as they are without form. This is the same concept within our spiritual life. If we do not allow God to impregnate us with his spirit, we are nonexistent Christians, nameless within the Book of Life (Matt 5:13).

Even for those who embody the spirit of God, we often may feel stillborn, once having life, experiencing spiritual death. Unfortunately, this happens to most Christians. On our journey, there are times when we will feel our spiritual health declining. It may feel like an infectious disease attempting to "kill, steal, and destroy" every divine cell in our bodies. However, the God of Glory is our strength (Ps 89:17). He is a spiritual heart defibrillator that prevents us from sudden death. "He gives power to the weak, and to those who have no might he increases strength" (Isa 40:29 King James 2000 Bible). When we are clothed in his glory, we are covered by the Father's power and might. We are dressed and prepared for battle. We have the authority to preach the gospel, to cast down demons, stand against Satan, heal the sick, raise the dead, cause the blind to see, and the lame to walk (Mark 16:15–18). We have God's permission, but our own limitations often plague us.

Truthfully, we are limited. Our physical bodies are feeble and deteriorate each day. No matter how youthful we may appear, we do not look as young as we did yesterday or the day before. The human body was not made to be supernatural, but it represents what we need for living on earth. Adam was created by the dust and given life through the breath of God. Without God's CPR, Adam wouldn't have been a living soul. Yet God's *consecrated powerful resurrecting* breath gave life, making Adam sacred to him, filling him with power, and restoring him from dust to life.

I Corinthian 15:45 states, "The first man Adam was made a living soul; the last Adam was made a quickening spirit." There were only two men in all the universe that were not made by human conception: Adam and Jesus Christ. Adam was created from the earth, but the last Adam, our Savior, was made by the spirit. Jesus was made into flesh only by the glory of God

(John 1:14), and this same glory was able to resurrect him from the dead. As children of the Highest God, the glory of the Father continues to rest upon us, raising us from sin to walk in a renewed way of life (Rom 6:4-6)

Fortunately, this new life is not limited to earth, but we will gain life in Heaven. Romans 6:8 states, "Now if we be dead with Christ, we believe that we shall also live with him." Living with the Savior means living in a newly made body as flesh and blood cannot inherit the kingdom of God. Our flesh is sinful, full of corruption and immorality (1 Cor 15:50), yet the glory of God will create for us a new body free from disease, embarrassment, and pain. A body that will be made to live forever. Unlike our current bodies, which are weak and sickly, these bodies will be full of glory and full of strength (1 Cor 15: 43-49). Our earthly bodies become frail and decay; however, we can rest assured that the Father of Glory will create a heavenly body suitable for our heavenly home.

Amazingly, God thinks of everything we need before we can conjure it in our minds. His provisions go beyond death into eternal life. If we believe that God will provide a new body in heaven, then we should also have faith that his provisions will happen here on earth. Sometimes our faith wavers, and we may wonder if God even hears our cry for help. However, we should have comfort in knowing that the Father knows what we need before we even ask of him (Matt 6:8). As children of God, we have immediate contact with him through prayer. No longer do we need a high priest to intercede on our behalf. However, we have access to the Highest of Priest, who listens to our request.

God listens, but are we speaking. Our heavenly Father desires to hear from his children, just like a natural parent. Parents tend to get anxious when they don't hear from their babies, causing their minds to be plagued with worry, as they reluctantly think the worst. How does God react when we are silent towards him? Does He pace the floors of heaven like a worried father, wondering if our love has waxed cold? Or does he send obstacles to rattle our attention, forcing us to pray? God is not an absentee father and wants to be involved in every part of our lives.

Developing a relationship with God starts by developing a daily prayer life. Prayer is the key to unlocking the mysteries of God (Jer 33:3). No man will fully understand his ways, but we can strive to know more of him. Both Jesus and Apostle Paul had a unique relationship with God as they were men of prayer. When the Sons of Sceva attempted to exorcise a demon, the evil spirit spoke back, saying, "Jesus I know, and Paul I know, but who are ye" (Acts 19:15)? Our relationship should be so enmeshed that even the demons see our resemblance to our Father. Just as God did with Job, we want him to testify to our faith and commitment towards him (Job 1:8). Nevertheless, if our relationship lacks, then so does the power. It does not profit us to be powerless Christians; however, we must revive our relationship with God through effectual fervent prayers (Jas5:16).

Praying is simply talking to our Father, yet this may seem easier said than done. Our churches are filled with mighty prayer warriors, and it is also filled with intimidating ministers who use elaborate words attempting to move the congregation. Jesus warns against being hypocritical prayers (Matt 6:5-7), as their words only move hot air and not the throne of God. Our prayer should touch the very heart of our Father, not by our extravagant words, but by our sincerity and expectancy. Often, we are so bogged down by the cares of life we do not even know where to begin. However, the beauty of the Spirit is that it will make intercessions for God's children even when we do not know how to pray (Rom 8:26-27). Not only this but, Jesus has given us a model prayer that we can use during times of distress through, *The Lord's Prayer* (Matt 6:9-13).

This prayer starts by saying, *"Our Father which art in Heaven."* The first line of this prayer makes the connection that God is indeed our heavenly Father, indirectly indicating that we are his spiritual children. *"Hallowed be your name, your kingdom come, Your will be done on earth as it is in heaven"* is a reference to God's name being holy on earth as well as in heaven. By acknowledging this, we accept the will of God, whether it serves the church (the earth) or the kingdom (heaven). *"Give us today our daily bread"* means we ask for our basic needs as well as the *Bread of Life*. *"And forgive us our trespasses, as we forgive those who trespass against us"* reveals our iniquity, yet it also discloses our willingness to forgive those who infringe upon us. *"Lead us not into temptation but deliver us from evil."* This passage of the Lord's Prayer is the supplication for righteousness. The Father understands we war against the deeds of the flesh (Gal 5:19-21). Therefore, we seek God to keep our evil mindset under subjection by the Spirit. *"For thine is the kingdom, the power, and the glory, for ever and ever"* recognizes God as the supreme ruler who rules with power and is lifted in glory from everlasting to everlasting. *Amen.* It merely means "so be it."

Our Amen puts an official stamp of approval of God being Father of all. A saying states, "Any man can make a child; it takes a real man to be a father." God did not only create us; however, he is the ultimate Father that loves, protects, and provides for his children. It is his good pleasure to make available every good thing we desire here on earth. He said, ask and it shall be given, seek and, you will find; knock, and it will be opened (Matt 7:7). These promises are reserved for the children of God who keep his commandments. If we don't, we become illegitimate, not resembling the Father. Our spiritual goal should be to bear the true likeness of God. He created us in his image, but it is our divine choice to represent his spirit. All God wants is the acknowledgment that He is our Father. Once we accept that, we can run into his arms like devoted children. We have an everlasting covenant with him, who deemed us worthy, not because of who we are but by who he is: God, the Father.

Chapter 5

GOD, THE SON

And lo a voice from heaven, saying, "This is my beloved Son, in whom I am well pleased."

MATT 3:17

LIVING IN A SMALL town, Ella longed for adventure. She wanted to break free of her mundane life and decided to follow the man of her dreams. Even though there was no promise of marriage, she was willing to leave the only home she knew. Placing the last of her items in her suitcase, a cry in the distance prevented Ella from continuing: "prepare to meet your God." Flabbergasted, she thought she was dreaming but soon realized it was a young girl with a band of church-goers ministering in the neighborhood. Relieved but reluctant, she opened the door to the persistent crowd, half-heartedly agreeing to attend that night's revival. Unbeknown to her, she would not make her planned trip. That very night God would deliver her soul. For the next seventy-years, Ella would become a well-known prayer warrior in the community she eagerly tried to escape.

Ever been in Ella's shoes, thinking life would go one way, but it went the other? "We may make our plans, but God has the last word" (Proverb 16:1 GNT). God will cancel our plan to fulfill his divine purpose in our lives. Admittedly, this interruption can be disrupting, frustrating, and a little inconvenient, especially when we consider the time and money spent planning. Then God comes along, throwing a powerful monkey wrench derailing our goals. Perhaps God didn't get the memos that our plans are essential to us. Maybe we didn't get the message that his plan trumps any and every ruse we can conceive. Even though it may leave us distraught and upset, "God's plan will always be greater and more beautiful than our disappointments."

No one knew this better than King David. What a devastating blow he received after God declined his request to build the temple. If anyone could make a resting place for our Lord, it was indeed him. After all, God said he was a man after his own heart (I Sam 13:14; Acts 13:22), which meant his request was pure with good intentions. Nevertheless, God had other plans for him. Facing defeat, David could have easily walked away or worse; he could have disregarded God and built the temple anyway. Instead of being shaken by God's no, David praised him for the future, yes. God knew the temple would ultimately be destroyed as earthly possessions and kingdoms come and go. However, his kingdom would reign forever. Through David's family, he would bring forth his Son to be the everlasting King causing David's house to be established for eternity (2 Sam 7:16).

The genealogy of Christ is recorded twice within the new testament. Even though there are a few discrepancies between Matthew and Luke's accounts, Jesus was certainly in David's lineage. In Revelation, Jesus confirms this saying, "I am the root and the offspring of David" (22:16). Within Matthew's Gospel, the genealogy acknowledges that Christ is the son of David, who is the son of Father Abraham (Matt 1:10). Luke's interpretations began with God, then Adam (Luke 3:38).

Interestingly, Luke's record is that he refers to Adam as the earthly son of God. Noticeably, the word son is lowercased to distinguish between the first and the *Last Adam*, Jesus Christ. The human vessel of God conceivably started with Adam to Abraham from David to Joseph. However, the spiritual genealogy of Jesus is incalculable as he was in the beginning with his Father. In this reference, Jesus was not created by God but existed with him even before the start of time.

John prophetically proclaims that "all things were made through him, and without him, nothing was made that was made" (John 1:3). Later confirmed by Paul, who stated that Jesus Christ created all things within the heavens and earth (Col 1:16–17). Yet, one of the most telling Scriptures is when Jesus prays for himself, asking the Father to restore the glory he once had with him at the beginning of the world (John 17:5). Scripturally acknowledging that Jesus Christ was with God before the world formation, thus in the beginning, full of glory and power.

Non-Christian believers are often unable to fathom the mysteries of the birth of Jesus Christ. Several scholars have sought historical evidence concerning his existence, while others cannot conceive he was born of a virgin birth. Then some believe there was a man called Jesus, but not a god. Perhaps it is easier for those intellectuals to trust in factual evidence versus hearing the true unadulterated word despite the accurate suggestions from historical characters conferred not only in the biblical text but historical content. Pontius Pilate and Apostle Paul's existence was proven through archaeological findings, yet no authentic artifacts have been found to support the presence of Jesus Christ. Arguably, both men encountered Christ, therefore, disputing the claim of his absence in history. Even though numerous scholars have recognized the existence of Jesus Christ, many cannot apprehend the wonder of his being.

Possibly, this is due to the unscientific way Christ entered the world. Conception comes by the fertilization of the female egg by the male sperm. There is no other systematic method in which a female of any species can conceive a child without joining both cells together. Biologically, through conception, both the male and female will provide chromosomes, which carries genetic information regarding their offspring's physical characteristics. Since the genes come from the father and the mother, they will undoubtedly have significant features like their parents. Still seemingly the case for our Lord and Savior. When the Holy Spirit impregnated Mary, it produced a child that was both flesh and divine, making him the *Son of Man* and the *Son of God*.

During biblical times, the term *son of man* was used as a synonym for human beings. Before Jesus entering the world, the Israelites used this title within the old testament to individualize man's characteristics. Job used this name to display man's weakness (Job 35:8) while in Psalms (80:16–18), it demonstrated man's strength. Ezekiel and Daniel were both called the Son of man (Ezek 2:3; Dan 8:17). However, the lettering changes. When God refers to them as the Son of man, the word *Son* is capitalized, and *man* is lowercased. Capitalizing the word *Son* does not mean that these men were Jesus incarnate, yet it distinguishes them as being filled with the Spirit of God to provide apocalyptical prophecies. During Daniel's vision, he witnessed the *Son of Man*, in which both words have been capitalized to display Jesus' human side and recognize his spiritual nature

Although Jesus was divine, he still underwent a typical life cycle. Just like all human life begins with conception, Jesus grew in his mother's womb. The Bible lets us know he was born in a manger (Luke 1:26–27), developed in stature from childhood (Luke 2:40) into adulthood (Luke 3:23), and then later died (Matt 27:35–38). While on earth, Jesus was still subjected to physical and emotional needs as the Bible provides information that he ate, slept, rejoiced, and mourned. As a human being, there was nothing different in comparison to our lives except Jesus Christ was without sin (Heb 4:15).

Conceivably, there was no sin found in Jesus because he resembled his Father. God cannot sin because he is holy, and since Jesus is his Son, he too is without sin. First Peter 2:21–24 provides a portrait of a perfect Savior. Even though Jesus was flesh in nature, he allowed the Holy Spirit to regulate his mind, body, and soul. In this manner, Jesus imitated his Father's spirit because he was his Son (John 5:19). This example shows we can also live a life free of sin. God granted this gift to us through and by the Holy Spirit, which is the same spirit that conceived Jesus in the womb. Being filled with the Spirit of God will make our lives seem like Jesus' human life. Though we are exposed to evil, we can sustain from sin if we have the spirit of God alive within us.

After Jesus' baptism, he encountered Philip, who proclaimed to Nathanael, "we have found the one Moses wrote about in the Law, and about whom the prophets also wrote – Jesus of Nazareth, *the son of Joseph*" (John 1:45). In this occurrence, both Philip and Nathanael recognized Jesus as the son of man, referring to him as Joseph's son. Indeed, Joseph acted as the natural father of Jesus and was subjected to obey him as all children honor their parents. However, in the same incidence, once Nathanael encounters Jesus, he quickly differentiates him from being Joseph's son to being the Son of God (John 1:49).

Even though Nathanael was quick to discern Jesus' identity, it appears that witnesses of his baptism still didn't believe, even after hearing the voice of the Lord. When John the Baptist christened Jesus, feasibly, they were not alone. Assumingly, others were there waiting to be baptized as John had several followers before Jesus (Mark 1:5). Not only this, but the Bible states that the Pharisees and the Sadducees came to the baptism as cynics (Matt 3:7). As Jesus came forth from the water, the Spirit of God descended on him like a dove, and a voice came from heaven, saying, "This is my *beloved Son*, in whom I am well pleased" (Matt 3:17). Despite hearing the voice of the Lord, confirming Jesus's identity, they still did not believe or want to recognize him as the Son of God.

At the moment of Jesus' baptism, it appeared that a transformation had occurred. The significance of the baptism shows a public agreement of obedience to God. It demonstrates a transition from death to life as our old sinful lives are symbolically buried to rise again, gaining eternal life (Col 2:12). When Jesus emerged from the Jordan River, God called him his Beloved Son. Calling Jesus beloved was a recognition of the start of his ministry and divine duty. This outward demonstration was an example for us, yet for God, it was an acknowledgment of Jesus' commitment to him. Due to his creation's sins, God grieved; but understood that the mourning would cease once his treasured Son spilled his precious blood for us. When Jesus went into the water, he was an "ordinary man" or merely the "son of man." However, when he resurfaced, the Spirit of the Living God rested on him, acknowledging that he is the beloved Son of God.

Jesus didn't have to leave his home in heaven, nor did he have to relinquish his rights to become his creation. However, because his love for his Father outweighed the love for himself, he willingly gave up everything. Perhaps this is one of the reasons why God called Jesus his beloved Son. Parents often sacrifice for their children; however, rarely does a child do it for their parents. Jesus understood that the only way to recover his Father's joy was to give his life as a ransom. God delighted in his affection that he confessed his love at Jesus' baptism for all to know that he was indeed, his Son.

Even though his disciples knew Jesus as the Son of God, he warned them to keep this information confidential (Matt 16:20). There were several reasons why Jesus advised against sharing his identity with others. First, he needed to start his ministry without rebellion. Imagine the rejection Jesus would have faced claiming to be the Son of God before establishing himself as human. This would have caused a premature uprising and ended his ministry before it could begin. Secondly, he needed his disciples to understand who he was fully. Even though Peter was the first to say he was the Son of God, he was also the first to speak against the suffering Jesus had to endure for our sake (Matt 16:16–23). Lastly, Jesus being the Son of God, had to be revealed and not told. Just as God had disclosed Jesus' identity to Peter, it had to be uncovered by the world.

Understanding that it was more important to be relatable versus identifiable, Jesus self-designated himself as the Son of Man. In our churches, self-exaltation often arises when leaders are easily offended by parishioners who do not call them by their correct titles. Speaking to the scribes and the Pharisees, Jesus warns them about self-glory as there is one higher than them (Matt 23). The discernable problem was not necessarily the title but the misuse and unwarranted glorification. Fraudulent names often lead to false hope and false praise. Consider a televangelist who claims to be a healer but only injures the believers' souls and wallets. Or one claiming to be a prophet, but their prophetic words are deceptive and counterfeit. Jesus' title as the Son of God wouldn't have amounted to much if he couldn't live up to his name. Appreciatively, with full humility, Jesus served us even unto death, demonstrating an unselfish nature that comes from his Father that only the Son of God could accomplish (Phil 2:8). Perhaps this is another example from Jesus to worry less about the title but do the work.

Jesus could have easily rested on his laurels, yet he allowed his works to establish him as the Son of God. As Jesus entered the city of Gadarenes, he witnessed an odd man living in the caves of the dead. In this chance meeting, we learn that the man's name is Legion because many demons possessed him. Amazingly, these unclean spirits recognized Jesus as the Son of God and fell at his feet and worshiped him, understanding that this power could only come by God (Matt 5:18; Luke 8:28). The same power caused the temple's curtain to tear, the earth to move, the rocks to break, and the dead in Christ to rise. On another occasion, after witnessing his authority, the Roman commander confessed that Jesus, indeed, was the Son of God (Matt 27:54). In both insistences, it appears that Jesus' actions, whether it be alive or in death, caused a divine acknowledgment of his identity.

Even though Jesus continues to prove himself, unbelief continues today as many false teachers dispute the eternal Sonship of Jesus Christ. One of the most recognizable Scriptures in all the Bible has caused some deception to his identity. John 3:16 states, "For God so loved the world, that he gave his only *begotten Son*"; taking the single word *begotten* into consideration, it means "to create or procreation.[1]" Therefore, many believe that Jesus was a construction of God without merely existing as an eternal being. However, the English literary term begotten comes from the Greek word *monogenes*, which means "pertaining to be the only one of its kind or class, unique in kind.[2]" This definition demonstrates the Godhead's uniqueness, including Jesus as the Son of God (John 1:14, 18; and 3:18).

1. "Begotten," lines 1–2.
2. Merritt, "What Does," lines 15–18.

God, The Son

God calling Jesus, his only begotten Son, distinguishes the exclusive relationship He possessed to this one supernatural being.

There is no relationship in all the universe, like God, the Father, and God, the Son. Jesus demonstrates this unique bond within the book of John, chapter 5. The first theme that arises is the continuing work that ensues between the Father and the Son. After he healed the lame man, the Jewish leaders rebuked him for working on the Sabbath as this was against the Mosaic Law. Even though the Son of God was born under the law (Gal 4:4), he also came to fulfill it (Matt 5:17). Years prior, Moses prophesied to the Israelites that God would raise a Prophet, like him, and they must heed to him (Deut 18:15). Therefore, Jesus refers back to Moses to confirm that he is the Prophet sent by God (John 5:46) to do the works of him that sent him (John 5:17).

Infuriating them even more, Jesus shows his unique relationship to God by saying that he and God are the same (John 5:18). No human or god can make that claim, yet this mere carpenter proclaimed this to the Jews. Jesus further exclaims that the works he performs are those in which his Father has achieved (John 5:19–21). Here, Jesus is making a simple case of heredity. God's omnipotent power does not merely transfer to Jesus but lives inside him because they are one. Jesus could only cast out demonic spirits (Matt 9:32–33), raise the dead (Luke 8:41–42; 49–56), and heal a man of a 38-year-old infirmity through the power of his Father (John 5: 1–4). However, despite witnessing these miracles, the Jewish leaders were filled with murderous rage; yet Jesus maintained his sonship with God (John 10:30–33).

God's love for his Son surpasses any love one could have for another, yet what greater love is there that he would allow him to die for us. Our relationship to the Father does not equate to his relationship with his Son, Jesus Christ. However, through the Spirit of Adoption, we have been made the sons and daughters of God, yet our association with him could only come by the Son (I John 4:9). Jesus gave his life for us, yet if we examine his identity, we can say, God, sacrificed himself for his creation. The unconditional love that God had for his Son was able to transfer to a sinful generation while allowing him to die for us without regret (Rom 5:8). It was God's eternal hope that we would accept his Son knowing full well that several would reject him. Nevertheless, Jesus' life, death, and resurrection would allow him to gain his equitable kingship over the universe.

Being the Son of Man and the Son of God, Jesus' life cycle went from existing in the beginning to becoming a human being, from being put to death and resurrected to reigning forever and ever more (Phil2: 6–8). Being divine and made of flesh, we can witness how our Lord mastered the two incomparable titles. As the Son of Man, he was able to undergo every temptation without yielding, empathizing with our weaknesses, and understand us as mere humans (Heb 4:15). However, being the Son of God allows him all authority in heaven and earth, through and by his Father (Matt 11:27). Just like a natural father gives his son a gift, God graciously gave Jesus this rule after he accomplished his divine task here on earth (Eph 1:10–23). As God's Son, Jesus allows him to have the power and wisdom of his Father (1 Cor 1:24). By this power, he will gain the status of king of all kings and lords of all lords. He will be known as the Wonderful Counselor, Mighty God, Everlasting Father, and Prince of Peace (Isa 9:6). Through his Father's power, Jesus' name has been placed before all other names as Jesus Christ, the Son of God.

Chapter 6

JESUS CHRIST: THE CHOSEN ONE

"Here is my servant, whom I uphold, my chosen one in whom I delight; I will put my Spirit on him, and he will bring justice to the nations"

ISAIAH 42:1

BEING CHOSEN BY GOD is one of the most significant accomplishments any person can attain without any effort. Think about politicians who campaign to become elected or those seeking job promotions working hard to advance. Those individuals work to get their positions, yet God does not choose because of our merits. He probably selects us because we lack them. As Christians, we are often plagued by why God would choose us to accomplish his works. However, the truthful answer is there is absolutely nothing special or exemplary that caused God to choose his Chosen. The reality is that we are as worthless as the dust we were made from, yet the Almighty God saw value in his creation despite our flaws. The only being chosen by God solely because of who he was, was his Son, Jesus Christ.

Arguments can be made that God chose several biblical characters because of their flawed identities. Saul was a man of great stature as he was the definition of "tall, dark, and handsome" (I Sam 9:2). He was the first-appointed king of Israel who had great success. However, his appearance did not mesh well with his leadership skills causing him to disobey God and ultimately take his own life (I Sam 31:4).

The succeeding king, David, did not look like a leader as he was the least of his father's seven sons. Nevertheless, God chose him because of his heart (I Sam 16:7). This was the same heart; however, that also broke half of God's commandments as a liar (2 Sam 11: 7–8), murder (2 Sam 11:17), adulterer (I Sam 11:4), coveter, and thief (2 Sam11:3, 2 Sam 12:9). David's appearance did not resemble a king, but his heart still resembled God's regardless of his character flaws. Even though his heart was towards God, he was still an imperfect sacrifice that could not be used to redeem man.

The redemption of God's creation had to be a flawless specimen to save the world. The origins of Jesus' name comes from the Hebrew name Yeshua, which is the abbreviated version of Yehoshua[1]. This name translates to the English name Joshua meaning "Yahweh is salvation.[2]" The two root names within Yehoshua is the prefix "Yeho" and the suffix "shua." Yeho is derived from God's Tetragrammaton name, Yod-He-Vav-He (YHVH) or Yahweh, which was previously established to mean Lord, only confirming his title[3]. However, Yeshua's prefix results from the Hebrew name *Yasha* which means "to deliver, save, or rescue,"[4] establishing his mission. Combining the prefix and suffix meanings it converts to "the Lord delivers, saves, and rescues," confirming his obligation as Savior.

The latter part of his name, Christ, comes from the Greek term *christos*[5], which means "to anoint." In Hebrew, the name is *mashiyach*, known in English translations as a messiah, which means "the anointed or the chosen one.[6]" This name is often used as a surname for the Son of God as well as a title. When Andrew encountered Jesus, he excitedly ran to find his brother Simon proclaiming, "we have found the *Messiah*" or the Christ (John 1:41). Andrew's proclamation was identifying Jesus' title as the Chosen One of God. However, later in Scripture, the name becomes attached to the forename, forming the name Jesus Christ (1 Cor 1:10; Acts 16:18; & Eph 5:20). Indeed, Christ is not a familiar last name, which is often classified by heredity. However, given the circumstances, it does represent his familial identity as the chosen vessel of God.

1. Parke, "Yeshua," lines 23–24.
2. "Joshua," lines 6–7.
3. "The Hebrew," lines 16–19.
4. Parke, "Yeshua," lines 21–22.
5. "What does Christ," lines 5–6.
6. "What does Christ, " lines 6–7.

Jesus Christ: The Chosen One

Within the old testament, the messianic prophecies foretold a Messiah who would deliver his people from their enemies. Unfortunately, many only saw Jesus's arrival as a tangible outcome without imparting the spiritual implications. At the onset of Christ, the Jews were subjected to the Roman Empire. Many believed the prophets when they foretold of a great deliverer. Yet, they thought this deliverer would physically extinguish their enemies versus spiritually freeing them from the yoke of bondage. This belief caused many to reject the Son of God as they looked beyond the underlying requirement for salvation but instead looked for an instant noticeable victory. Unable to realize that their foremost rival was not Rome but Satan, they misunderstood the real mission of Jesus Christ.

As the elect of God, Jesus came to destroy Satan's power and demolish sin from the world (Hebrew 2:14-15). Within the Garden of Eden, evil crept into existence as the serpent tempted God's creation to disobey him. As sin entered, so did death and the inability to maintain eternal life. This lurking immorality caused a great divide among God's people triggering abomination, idolatry, and hatred within the land that God created. However, before the serpent could slither away, the Lord assured him that one day he would be trampled by the perfect offspring (Gen 3:17). That offspring would be Jesus Christ, who would fulfill the messianic prophecies to take away the world's sins (I John 3:5). On the cross, Jesus accomplished his Father's promise by tasting death for us so we could gain everlasting life (Heb 2:9).

He came to fulfill the law and the prophecies spoken of him several years prior (Matt 5:17). One of the first messianic prophecies occurred was when God said he would bless Abraham and Jacob's lineage to produce a *Star* that would one day destroy all their enemies (Num 24:17). Many believed that this star was David since many of God's enemies were defeated during his reign (2 Sam 8:2; Ps 60:1-12). However, the ultimate shining light is Jesus Christ, who will defeat all of God's enemies within the last days. Isaiah also prophesied about the coming of the Messiah who would be born of a virgin birth (7:14), would bring forth joy and blessings (12:3), heal every disease (35:5-7), and would call all to repentance (43:16-28). Through his birth, he accomplished several of the prophecies; however, more needed to be achieved.

One of which was revealing his identity as Christ. Proving that he was God's chosen elect was no easy feat considering that he was an ordinary man born of ordinary people. After Jesus performed the miracle of feeding the multitude with two small fish and five loaves, he spoke to his disciples concerning being the Bread of Life. Overhearing this conversation, many questioned his claim stating, "is not this Jesus, the son of Joseph, whose father and mother we know?" (John 6:42). Jesus acknowledges their inquiries. Nevertheless, they were still unable to recognize Jesus as the Chosen One of God.

In our own lives, people may not acknowledge our position change in him despite God elevating us in our ministries. Like the Jews who confronted Christ, they may also question our titles simply because they know our family or our previous background and possible sins. However, our mortal beings are genetic and are connected to our biological parents, yet our spiritual man comes from our heavenly Father.

On another occasion, Jesus asked Peter who he was, and he replied, "*The Christ of God*" (Luke 9:20). Matthew and Mark recorded this conversation within the new testament in which Peter's response referred to Jesus as the Christ or the Messiah (Matt 16:15–16, Mark 8:27–29). However, in the third recording, Luke states that Peter's response was The Christ of God. One could argue that this title is slightly different from being the Messiah as it personalizes that Jesus is the sole chosen vessel from God. In Matthew's and Mark's accounts, Peter's response as Jesus being The Christ is the title of Jesus. Yet Luke's recording specifies who *gave* him this exclusive name. Throughout time, there were many people that God had elected to accomplish his divine will. However, being the "Chosen of God" is quite different than being chosen by God.

There is no dispute that John the Baptist was chosen by God, causing many to believe that he was the promised Messiah. Jesus himself even recognized the greatness in him (Matt 11:11). Before his birth, no prophetic words were spoken for nearly four hundred years, and no miracles were done within the last five hundred. One of the first signs of a miracle occurred when John the Baptist's parents produce a child in their old age. This phenomenon caused many to wonder if this child would be the Messiah. Another misleading assumption was that John the Baptist was the incarnation of Elijah confusing many to think he was the selected one from God.

Prior to John the Baptist's birth, he would be filled with the Holy Spirit and possess Elijah's spirit and power (Luke 1:17). When people witnessed John the Baptist's baptisms and message, they intuitively knew something was unique about this simple man, which caused the Pharisees to question if he was the Messiah, Elijah, or the Prophet (John 1:24–25). A few theologians continue to ponder if Jesus confirmed that John the Baptist was indeed Elias or Elijah (Matt 11:12–14), however little dispute is made that Jesus was the chosen Messiah.

As the Christ of God, Jesus was the chief designated vessel that God chose to accomplish his divine will. The will of God had to be perfected by a perfect being. There were great prophets, kings, and disciples within the Bible, but none were without their character flaws. Noah was a man of virtue but was an alcoholic (Gen 9:20–21). Solomon was the wisest of all men but was deceived by his wives, losing sight of God (1 Kgs 11). Moses was considered the most humble man on earth (Num 12:3) yet was subjected to anger and even killed a man (Exod 2:11–12).

We are perfectly imperfect. It appears that God selects flawed individuals to accomplish his will; however, the ultimate sacrificial lamb could not be defective. God recognized the imperfections of his people and realized that a new covenant was needed for divine restoration. The previous law demonstrated what we must do; however, under the new covenant, the grace of God shows us how to achieve it (John 1:17). Through and by the shedding of Jesus's innocent blood, the new covenant was established, providing us the gift of eternal life and atonement for sin (Eph 2:8–9).

As the Messiah, Jesus' ministry was to call all sinners to repentance (Mark 2:17). Repentance is more than being apologetic, yet it involves a change of behavior. The Greek word for repent is "metanoeo" with the two root words being "meta" and "noeo." *Noeo* refers to a person's mind and thoughts as *meta* means "movement or change."[7] Therefore, when Jesus called for repentance, he was merely asking everyone to change their mindsets. Paul confirmed this notion when he said, "And be not conformed to this world, but be ye transformed by the renewing of your mind" (Rom 12:2). Repentance brings forth a transformation from one behavior to another (2 Cor 5:17).

When Jesus entered the home of Zacchaeus, he was a recognizable sinner among the citizens of Jericho. He was a tax collector who perhaps defrauded many people to accrue his wealth. Nevertheless, after one encounter with Jesus, Zacchaeus sorrowfully acknowledged his sins. Ultimately, giving half of his possessions to the poor and repaying those he cheated four times the amount he took (Luke 19:5–8). Zacchaeus' change of heart is an example of why Jesus came to earth to free us from sin.

---

7. "Repentance," lines 14–17.

Despite criticism, Jesus had an assignment to fulfill. When Jesus saw Zacchaeus, he called him by name and said, "come down; for today I must abide at thy house." What was amazing is that Zacchaeus was looking for Jesus, but Jesus was looking for him. Jesus had an assignment to bring salvation to Zacchaeus' home that very day. Salvation could have come to anyone as he passed through Jericho; however, the appointment was for Zacchaeus. Sometimes, God will save the most unlikely person to get everyone's attention. Zacchaeus was a con man; nevertheless, after meeting Jesus, he was instantly saved from his iniquities.

The saving grace of God allows us to be rescued from the penalization of sin, which meant that Jesus had to give his life as a ransom to redeem us from the state of our wickedness (Matt 20:28). God's intention for his children was everlasting life, but sin caused death to cheat us of our inheritance. Therefore, God sent his Son to free us from the bondage of sin. Jesus came to preach to those who were brokenhearted, sick, and captive (Luke 4:18–19). We all fall into one of these categories, experiencing emotional and physical impairments as well as imprisonment. Even though some of us may not have experienced actual incarceration, we still were or currently are captives to sin. Yet, through the redeeming blood of Jesus Christ, we were bailed out to be free (John 8:36).

Unfortunately, like our judicial system, we have some repeat offenders in our churches who, despite being released from the enemy's snares, chose to return to imprisonment. It often boggles the mind to think of someone who was once free returning to bondage, yet this is the case for many Christians. Being enslaved to sin is a state of oppression as well as servitude. Many believe that penal labor is equivalent to modern-day slavery unless the grace of the state pays inmates. Ironically, this is equivalent to spiritual suppression. Those enslaved to Satan work towards death, receiving these wages for their works of iniquity (Rom 6:23). Only by God's grace can they be rehabilitated to do good works freeing them from spiritual bondage.

Within our judicial system, habitual offenders return to prison to serve a life sentence based upon our government's three-strike rule. Gratefully, our God does not give us a limitation on repentance (Lam 3:21–23). He can restore the most horrendous criminal, the worst sinner, or the most dishonest hypocrite. He is a God of mercy that allows us to choose life or a death sentence. We all one day will serve an eternal judgment; however, it's best to be entirely arrested in God versus being detained by the devil.

Jesus Christ: The Chosen One

As our *Redeemer*, Jesus Christ has freed us from the yoke of bondage through and by his precious blood (Eph 1:7). The first signs of redemption started during Moses' time when he commanded each household to sacrifice a lamb. Ironically, this act of redemption foreshadowed how the Lamb of God would become the ultimate sacrifice for our sins. The Israelites applied the blood of the lamb on the door to escape "the destroyer" (Exod 12:11), and likewise, we apply the blood of the Lamb to our lives to escape eternal death. Within this new covenant, Jesus used his blood in order to possess eternal redemption, meaning that our past, present, and future sins have been forgiven through our sincere repentance (Heb 9:11–15)

The Bible is divided into two parts: the old testament and the new testament. Ironically, this could also mean the old covenant and the new covenant. Under the old testament, God made a contractual agreement with the Israelites to be his chosen people, and they were given over six hundred laws to follow. If a person sinned against these laws, then animal sacrifices were established to atone for sins. During this time, atonement occurred once a year, in which the high priests were only permitted into the Holy of Holies to intervene on the people's behalf. However, the new testament is a new agreement between God and the believer. Under this new covenant, God doesn't merely provide laws. Instead, he gives over seven hundred promises through his Son Jesus Christ to include salvation from sin (Matt 1:21), blessings for persecution (Matt 5:11), physical healing (Matt 8:17), and rest for our souls (Matt 11:28). Galatians 4:4–5 also lets us know that we are blessed under the new testament to become the sons and daughters of God as he redeemed us from the Law.

Becoming a curse for us, Jesus restored the blessings of Abraham to the Gentiles "so that we would receive the promise of the Spirit through faith" (Gal 3:13–14). One of the first agreements between God and Abraham was based on an act of faith and obedience (Gen 12:1–3). Abraham left his home to follow God, and in return, God would make him a great nation. Due to Abraham's faith, God promised that he would also justify him, which meant the promise to forgive any and all his past, current, and future sins (Gen 15:6). These blessings also pertain to us as we are Abraham's seed.

Abraham and Sarah's true descendants are not of biological ancestry; however, they are by the Spirit. Those who exhibit faith and obedience to God are the great nation that God promised within the Abrahamic covenant (Rom 9:7–8; Gal 3:7). The original promises given to the Jews under the old testament also have been given to God's chosen elect (2 Cor 1:20).

Just as God justified Abraham, he validates us by the redeeming power of the blood of Christ. We are no longer enslaved to sin as God made a covenant to forgive our transgressions. We all have sinned, but we are now redeemed (Rom 3:23–24).

Lytrosis is the Greek word for redeemed, which means "a ransoming, deliverance, or a rescue.[8]" In biblical times, those captured in battle would be taken as prisoners. Notification of their apprehension would be told to their families to be released for a price. Astonishing, there is no greater warfare than the one we fight against our adversary. As sin entered the world, it spread like cancer, consuming many to death separating us from eternal life (Isa 59:2). This void caused the creation of God to become prisoners of war. It was not in God's plan for his children to remain imprisoned by sin; therefore, redemption was essential. For this plan to work, a ransom had to be given: one life, for all life.

Our redemption was paid with the highest of cost, the cost of our Savior's blood. Nevertheless, our Lord and Savior, Jesus Christ, paid the costly price. His receipt is the nail prints in his hand. The invoice is the wound on his side. We no longer have to be enslaved to sin, for he paid it all at Calvary. The redeemed of the Lord will say it is so, for they were rescued from the hand of the enemy (Ps 107:2).

Our rescue was all because of the *Risen Savior*, who died for our sins, was buried, and then rose again (I Cor 15:3–4). Jesus was appointed to die, but most importantly, the children of God were to live. For us to live, we must first succumb to death. Indeed, this sounds contradictory, yet for us to rise in Christ, we must die. While Apostle Paul was teaching about the resurrection of Jesus Christ, he revealed that he dies daily (1 Cor 15:31). It appeared that some believers doubted life after death as naturally, it was implausible that a person who was dead could rise again. However, Paul reassures them that he and hundreds of witnesses saw the resurrected Christ (1 Cor 15:4-8), confirming the possibility of life after death.

Theologians have often argued that Paul's daily death means something more spiritually enlightening, like dying to his flesh. As believers, we should crucify our flesh every day (Gal 5:24). However, in this instance, it is believed that Paul was talking about the crumbling of his own natural body. Paul's résume of suffering was quite impressive as he was beaten repeatedly and escaped death on numerous occasions (2 Cor 11:29–28).

---

8. "Saving and Redeeming," lines 13–14.

Even though our bodies did not endure the hardship Paul tolerated, our bodies are also decaying. Our eyesight gets weaker, hearing becomes less audible, and our muscles become feeble. Growing older means our bodies deteriorate with every birthday. As morbid as it sounds, believers should rejoice in knowing that this brings us that much closer to gaining our resurrected bodies. Everyday living is yet another day closer to death. Often people do not want to think of their mortality, yet the good news is that we all have an appointment with death and when it comes, so will Christ (Hebrew 9:28).

Apostle Paul confessed that our outward man perishes every day, yet our spiritual man is renewed persistently (2 Cor 4:16). Admittedly, since we do not see our inward person, we tend to think of it less than our physical bodies. For example, we are quick to acknowledge bodily pain yet ignore the cries of our souls. Let's think about our last physical ailment; did we take medication, visit the doctor, or do whatever we could to heal the pain? We do everything to preserve our physical life. However, can we say the same for our spiritual man?

Examining ourselves, do we eat heartedly the word of God, strengthen ourselves with the holy Scriptures, and meditate on his word day and night? Afflictions will occur, whether it is physical, emotional, or psychological. However, Paul admonishes believers to think of our problems as light afflictions, which work towards a greater gain (verse 17). Regardless of the obstacles, we should focus on strengthening our spiritual selves. If we maintain our spirit man, then we will be able to trust in the Lord to deliver us out of all our troubles (Ps 34:17)

Our deliverance rest on Jesus Christ, who was chosen to deliver his people from sin (Gal 1:4), hindrances, and strongholds. Unfortunately, we tend to focus merely on the fact that Jesus is our *Deliverer* without fully understanding the origins of how to be delivered. Deliverance comes from complete openness with God. It seems that we are programmed to believe lies as our forefathers Adam and Eve believed the serpent's fabrications. However, it is one thing to accept someone else's lies, but it is another to consider your own.

As the body of Christ, we cannot be fully delivered because we hold fast to the untruths that we tell ourselves about ourselves. One of the biggest lies is, "I don't know what I need to be delivered from." We equate being delivered as being freed from sin, therefore putting on spiritual blinders to prevent seeing the other hindrances and weights we tend to stumble over.

Deliverance is an act of God in which He snatches us away from danger. But first, we must recognize that there is a threat. If we do not acknowledge that we are in jeopardy, then how can we be rescued? Naturally, if anyone is in danger, they immediately cry for help. Help allows the rescuer to take charge and release the individual from impending doom. However, if there is no cry for help, there is presumedly no need. God admonishes his people to come boldly to the throne of grace and confess our faults to him (Heb 4:16). Yet, if there is no confession, is there any true deliverance (Rom 10:10)?

One of the first acts of salvation is confession. First, we must confess our sins and then acknowledge that Jesus is Lord (Rom 10:9). Redemption cannot occur without these admissions, as the same can be said about deliverance. For the Chosen Vessel of God to deliver us, we must openly confess what holds us back from our relationship with God. Deliverance does not always equate to sin, but it does correlate to spiritual strongholds.

Ironically, a stronghold is a place of refuge and safety. Coincidently, many believers are hiding behind pseudo fortresses as some are afraid to be delivered. They tend to lie to themselves, finding false security and comfort in family, work, and finances. When we make these things our hiding place, God tends to crumble those frail walls. The only real salvation comes from our Lord and Savior, Jesus Christ. Therefore, to be genuinely delivered, confession is necessary.

As believers, our confidence is that the Lord hears our prayers (I John 5:14–15). His ears are always open to the cries of his people. Yet, we remain tight-lipped, holding on to our sins and weights as if it's some classified secret. The truth is God already knows about our problems. He is just merely waiting for us to confess them. Our complete acknowledgment brings forth deliverance. It is not only enough to say, "Lord, I've sinned" because we all have sinned, but we must specifically and directly call out those explicit offenses to God. Even though God already knows what hinders us, it's time that we recognize those weights within ourselves.

James admonished the children of God to confess our faults to one another (Jas5:16). Telling our sins to others cannot happen until we first admit them to God. Recognizing our weaknesses to him releases the chains that once kept us in spiritual bondage. Once we are freed, it becomes easier to testify to our sisters and brothers. By telling others about our deliverance, it strengthens our relationship with God as well as glorifies the Son. Confessing our flaws to one another also helps others witness the power of God. Some people may not fully believe the conversion of the biblical characters, yet it is more straightforward for them to accept the changes in us. By doing this, many will see the Father and Son's true identity through our mere confession.

Unfortunately, in the last days, many people will come in Jesus' name, saying that they are the sent messiah; however, we must not be misled (Matt 24:4–5). Timothy warns the people of God that "evil men and imposters will grow worse and worse, deceiving and being deceived" (2 Tim 3:13). Deception will come to the world, defrauding many of their birthrights. We are the heirs to the Kingdom of Heaven, but spiritual scam artists will arise performing miracles confusing even God's elect. Safeguarding ourselves from these cons will be no easy task. Therefore, as believers, we must fully understand God's ways as his Son derives from him and the false prophets from their father, which is Satan.

Knowing God's Word will help us decipher those who were sent and those who went. Jesus tells us to examine their character (Matt 7:15–20). A false prophet will promote themselves seeking power, fortune, and fame. These individuals will have the form of godliness but deny the power of God (2 Tim 3:5). However, Jesus never endorsed himself based upon the miracles he performed but always acknowledged the Father. Workers of iniquity will do the opposite, attempting to claim their praise. Unfortunately, these false prophets will be self-glorified, ultimately deceiving many from the mission of God. For us to resist these false witnesses, we must arm ourselves with the knowledge of God and his son Jesus Christ.

As God's Chosen One, Jesus came to save the lost (Luke 19:1–10), to forgive sins (Matt 26:26–29), and to heal all diseases (Matt 4:23). However, one of the primary goals was to restore life to his children (John 10:10). Offering life to us meant that God had to deliver his Son to death. Through this mission, God sent a Messiah, a Redeemer, and a Deliverer to accomplish what seemed like a mission impossible. Yet without thought of his own life, Jesus willingly accepted the task to live for us and then die for our sins. God accomplished his plan for redemption by selecting his Son, Jesus Christ, as his Chosen Vessel.

Chapter 7

JESUS CHRIST, THE SAVIOR

For unto you is born this day in the city of David a Saviour, which is Christ the Lord.

LUKE 2:11

SYMBOLS WERE USED IN ancient times to convey meaning without the written or spoken word. Historically, early man used pictographs, like the Egyptians, who used hieroglyphics as their formal writing system[1]. These images were used to represent significant events such as wars, and the king's dynasty reigns. During medieval times, families used a coat of arms or a family crest that used several symbols to represent their heritage. Today, logos are everywhere, from hearts to express love to crossbones to mean death. Symbolism helps each culture summarize meaning into one simple image. Americans understand our flag's symbols: the thirteen stripes represent the first original colonies, the fifty stars signifying the states, and the colors embody our purity, bravery, and justice system[2]. These symbols provide ideologies that give us a foundation, which often shapes our thoughts and behaviors.

In biblical times, the cross represented a brutal, ruthless punishment for all to witness. Romans used crucifixion to publicly warn others of the

1. Mark, "Ancient," lines 14–19.
2. "The History," lines 21–23.

Jesus Christ, The Savior

danger that would befall them if they broke the law. Since death was not immediate, the individual hung there openly humiliated, which sent others a lasting message[3]. Symbolically, the cross served as a gruesome, humiliating symbol that the Romans hoped would convey their message to their political rivals. However, with the death of Jesus, the meaning of the cross changed from death to life. No longer do we see the humility, but the victory. A symbol that was once used to frighten with death now encourages life.

Another symbol that is widely utilized is the fish. Undoubtedly, the fish symbol has been distinguished as a Christian image, yet what does it truly mean. Lchthys is the Greek word for fish, which serves as an acronym to the phrase "Iesous Christos Theou Huios Soter.[4]" The name translates to "Jesus Christ, Son of God, Savior," which recognizes the three unique titles of our Lord. This symbol means means that Jesus Christ is the Messiah who was sent by his Father to save the world. Coincidently, the first disciples in which Jesus called were fishermen, who he would use to convey his message to those who needed to be saved. When Jesus met Peter, he told him that he would make him fishers of men showing forth his authority as the Christ, the Son of God, and *the Savior* (Matt 4:19).

Fishing is a patient sport, often causing those holding their rods to wait patiently for hours. When fishers cast their bait, most times, the fish are unseen. Yet the fisherman continues to sit there in the hopes he will make a catch. As the ultimate fisher of men, Jesus Christ waits patiently for sinners to take hold of his love to reel them in his safety net. Luke 19:10 states, "For the Son of Man came to seek and to save what was lost." Like the invisible fish that are adrift in the sea, without Jesus, we are lost in the world. God sent his Son to rescue us from a state of wandering in despair to regain hope in him. Without salvation, we are lost in sin, drowning in an ocean of disappointment, shame, and guilt. However, we were not invisible to God. He saw us in our misplaced state of helplessness and sent forth a Life Savior that would rescue us out of our despair.

The Lord's net is wide enough to catch every individual who wants to be entangled in him. No one can come to Jesus unless God draws him into salvation (John 6:44). This verse is controversial, as many have contemplated the meaning behind the word *draw*. It appears that if God draws individuals to him, then he chooses explicitly those he wants to serve him.

3. Ehrman, "Why Romans," lines 24–32.
4. Lungin, "Explanation," lines 1–8.

This is not true as it is the Father's will that no one would perish. Therefore, God does not call only a few to salvation.

Before he spoke about the drawing, he first performed the miracle of the two fish and five bread loaves. After witnessing this event, the crowd followed him to Capernaum, not because of the miracle, but perhaps wanting additional food. Despite observing God's power, the people begin to murmur about Jesus seeing only an ordinary man who proclaimed to be the source of everlasting life. Often, unbelievers will testify unknowingly to miracles without recognizing the real power of God. Instead of seeing the miracle as a blessing, they see it as pure luck. Unfortunately, this was the drawing or the bait that was set. Instead of recognizing God, they take the opportunity to swim around the net.

God draws us into salvation by using different methods for different individuals. Just like fish, some bait works for some, while another works for others. For some Christians, their childhood knowledge of God may have drawn them closer to him, while it took some people tragedies. Others may find themselves tired of their mundane lives and sought for something higher than them. Then there are some who God spoke to do his will personally. Regardless of the situation that occurs in all of us, God draws all men towards him.

Oddly enough, some people are attracted to what God can provide them instead of the lasting impacts of salvation. As Jesus spoke to the crowd, he declared, "I am the bread of life. Whoever comes to me will never go hungry, and whoever believes in me will never thirst again" (John 6:35). The people sought Jesus, not because he was their everlasting Savior, but he was an instant source for their natural need. Seeking out Jesus for food is equivalent to some believer's self-styled devotion to God. These individuals seek after the blessings versus the lifestyle of holiness. They tend to follow Jesus when convenient for them, rather than following him on a continued basis. By proclaiming to be the *Bread of Life,* Jesus acknowledged that he is an eternal source to meet our needs, not just for today, but tomorrow, and forever.

Bread is a primary dietary necessity that provides many nutrients that are beneficial to our survival. Bread is the most widely consumed food in the world. They serve bread first at many restaurants as it helps fill the person before eating, allows them satisfaction as they wait, and welcomes customers to their establishment. Similarly, as the Bread of Life, Jesus is a necessary life requirement for our salvation, and he is the most widely known person on all the earth. As bread fills us, Jesus fills us with life. While we wait on deliverance, we have the assurance that we can partake of him to sustain us during our waiting period. Lastly, bread is considered comfort food, and knowing that Jesus Christ is the Bread of Life, allows us to have a spiritual comfort of salvation through him.

Withstanding from eating bread causes our bodies to be low in energy and impacts our mental cognition. Despite the low carb diet crave, bread is an essential part of our balanced diet. Therefore, Jesus being the Bread of Life is a vital part of our spiritual walk. We cannot cut him out of our spiritual diets, but we must partake of him daily and spiritually. In the spirit, we must feed ourselves with the Word of God. In the Lord's prayer, he says, "Give us this day our daily bread." Perhaps, he was referring to a request to provide for our basic day-to-day needs. However, our daily bread is also the Word of God. We must strengthen ourselves with it to become stronger and more devoted Christians.

During the last supper, Jesus broke bread and said, "This is my body, which is given for you. Do this in remembrance of Me" (Luke 22:19). This lasting ritual has been going on for centuries to remember our Lord and Savior, Jesus Christ. Partaking of his broken body helps us recall the events of his tormented death. Each time we take the bread, we should remember that it was only by his death that we can have everlasting life. Our Savior gave his life so that he could become the Bread of Life he offers to those who believe.

This bread comes straight from Heaven as Jesus is the *Bread of God* (John 6:33). Jesus told the congregation that the bread that Moses gave did fall from the sky, but it was not the real bread of heaven. The true *Bread of Heaven* was the one that was speaking to them (John 6:32). Once again, the people were missing God because they focused on their physical needs versus their spiritual requirements. Instead of requesting additional information about this life-giving bread, they ignorantly believed that manna would reappear this time, offering everlasting life.

Claiming to be the source of everlasting life caused discord among the Jews. It was difficult for them to believe that this ordinary man could claim to be the Son of God. When they challenged him, Jesus said, "Verily, verily, I say unto you, Before Abraham was, I am" (John 5:58). This was indeed a remarkable statement, which puzzled and infuriated the Jewish leaders. They could not comprehend that this young carpenter could announce that he was before Abraham and proclaimed to be the Son of God.

Abraham was an essential part of the Jewish doctrine and had existed years before Jesus. Nevertheless, Jesus made this declaration stating that He was undeniably, the "*I am.*"

Seven times within the new testament did Jesus prophetically claimed to be the "I am." As previously discussed, after Jesus fed the multitude, the people followed him. Upset with their motives, Jesus declared to be the Bread of Life. Jesus criticized the people's intentions as they desired a temporary fix; not knowing what Jesus offered would satisfy them forever. Often, people attempt to fill the voids in their lives with food, alcohol, drugs, poor relationships, and other vices, which only provide short-term gratification. Nevertheless, accepting Jesus as our personal Savior gives a lasting fulfillment that can seal our lives' hollow parts.

Evidence is provided in the book of John, chapter 8 of the adulterous woman. Infidelity often occurs when individuals seek after what they believe is lacking within their relationships. The woman caught in adultery was seeking something but found nothing that could bring true fulfillment. When she met Jesus, he freed her from empty pleasures and guided her in her darkest hour.

Jesus proclaimed to the crowd, "I am *the light of the world*: he that followeth me shall not walk in darkness but shall have the light of life" (John 8:12). It is difficult to search for anything in the dark. Jesus admonishes believers to walk in the light versus in the dark to ensure that we are on the right path (John 12:35). Sin is darkness, as it can be overpowering. Nevertheless, the darkness has never overpowered the light (John1:5). Jesus is that light, and no matter how much sin there is in a person's life, accepting Jesus will help illuminate their paths, leading them closer to him.

Jesus referenced himself as the good shepherd by saying, "*I am the good shepherd*: the good shepherd giveth his life for the sheep (John 10:11). As we follow Jesus, he will guide us like a good shepherd. A shepherd does not lead his flock into the darkness, for it is "full of terrors." Nevertheless, he will steer them towards those things which are good such as green pastures and still waters, leading them on a path of righteousness (Ps 23:1–2).

David, a mere shepherd boy, killed both a lion and a bear to save his father's sheep. David risked his life just for one lamb. Perhaps, this foreshadowed Jesus as being the good shepherd as Satan is a "roaring lion, seeking whom he may devour" (1 Pet 5:8). Our adversary seeks to single us out from the flock to destroy our relationship with Christ. However, Jesus being the good shepherd, came down from Heaven, gave up his life to save his Father's sheep.

This is one of the reasons why Jesus said, "*I am the resurrection and the life*: he that believeth in me, though he were dead, yet shall he live" (John 11:25-26). God's divine resurrecting power was the life delivering breath that was given back to his Son. Death had no dominion over Jesus as sin should have no authority over us. Jesus freely gave up his life, so we may also live without the fear of condemnation but in the knowledge of him. We must die to sin to gain eternal life. This is the reason why Paul said, "I want to know Christ and the power of his resurrection (Phil3:10). For us to be acquainted with Christ, we must deny the sin in our lives and wholeheartedly follow him. The resurrecting power allows us to become dead to sin and live in the fullness of Christ. Paul also believed, "it is a trustworthy statement: For if we died with him, we would also live with him" (2 Tim 2:11).

It was not God's intentions that we should die, yet it was the reward that we deserved for sin. The Old Testament's patriarchs indicate God's plans for everlasting life as Methuselah lived 969 years, and Noah lived 950 years. The longevity of man was cut short due to immorality and wickedness. God's proposal for redemption meant that his beloved Son would pay the ultimate cost. His precious blood had to be sacrificed so God's proper plan could be fulfilled. This plan brought forth God's forgiveness over sin as well as the power to overcome death. Through the death of Jesus Christ, God's children can inherit everlasting life.

To have a life free from death, we must understand that Jesus is the way to the Kingdom of Heaven. In John 14:6, Jesus said, "*I am the way, the truth, and the life*: no man cometh unto the Father, but by me." There is no other way that we can enter the Kingdom of Heaven but through Jesus. During the last supper, Jesus was preparing his disciples for his departure but assured them that (1) he was preparing a place for them; (2) he would see them again, and (3) he would be there with them (John 14:1-3).

Hundreds of years prior, Isaiah prophesied about this way of holiness (Isa 35:8). Jesus, himself stated that the "kingdom of heaven is like a treasure hidden in the field" (Matt 13:44). When Jesus told his disciples, "I am the way," he gave all believers the ultimate treasure map to their destination. Sin's heavy load cannot be taken on this journey as this way is too constricted for our flesh. Galatians 5:19-23 explains the sinful baggage we must leave behind, but it also gives the attributes we must possess on our way to Christ. Therefore, to pursue the ways of Christ, we cannot take our own bag. Nevertheless, we must unpack our spiritual suitcase, denying ourselves to follow him.

Jesus is the way, but he is also the foundation of truth and life. This is depicted by John's description of Jesus being the Word: "the Word became flesh and dwelt among us, and we have seen his glory, glory as of the only Son from the Father, full of grace and truth" (John 1:14). The personification of the term *word* showed the natural attributes of God dwelling in the flesh. God's Word came alive it regenerated grace to an unjust world. We did not deserve it, yet God gave us his favor. Not only did he give us this gift, but he gave us his Son, who is right because his Word is truth.

Life in God means that we must stand firm on integrity and remain connected to him. Jesus stated, "*I am the vine*, ye are the branches: He that abideth in me, and I in him, the same bringeth forth much fruit: for without me ye can do nothing" (John 15:5). To be successful in life, we must attach ourselves to the vine. In the natural sense, the vine is the source of growth as it entangles around the branches to provide water and nutrients for continued development. So it is within the spirit. Jesus gives us his word so we may grow in our Christian walk.

Without the vine, the branches will die, not achieving their purpose. Glorifying God means that we should live our lives to be productive citizens of the Kingdom. Daily, we should take inventory of our lives. Are we bringing forth good fruit, or are we good for nothing, needing to be cast away in a fiery pit? As believers, we must enmesh ourselves in Jesus to become victorious fruit producers in him. The only way that we can bring forth fruit is by staying connected to the vine.

We must stand firm on his word; without a strong foundation, we would crumble. When building a home, there are several steps a person must accomplish. First, they must find a vacant lot and complete a perk test to see if the soil can absorb the water. Once this is completed, they must start selecting a builder. There are several construction workers that a person can choose; however, they must choose one that will be effective. Sure, this process may be costly and lengthy. However, it will provide the best outcome. Lastly, the final step is securing a building permit. This permit allows the owner to start working on building their home.

Even though these are natural steps in construction, they can also be applied to our spiritual lives. God looks for a vacant lot where he can abide, ensuring that it is fertile ground that can produce good fruits (Matt 13:9).

However, before God can start building us up, we often must be broken down. Our brokenness is where we can find strength. God wants us to select him as the ultimate builder in our lives, but first, he needs our permission. God is simply asking, "Can I build here?" He wants to build our lives upon a foundation of hope, truth, and love. The only way to build a good foundation in God is to ensure that the *Chief Cornerstone* is held up: his Son, Jesus Christ.

How ironic is it that Jesus, who was seen as a mere carpenter, is now labeled as the Chief Cornerstone? The cornerstone, often called the foundation stone, is "the first stone set in construction.[5]" When this stone is set, it determines how the building will be constructed. This stone must be reliable as it connects and brings the other two walls together. In the spirit, the other two walls are God and the Holy Spirit. Without the Son, no man can see God, and without believing in him, the Holy Spirit cannot dwell. Unfortunately, Jesus was the cornerstone that was rejected (Ps 118:22). Rejecting Jesus also means that God and the Holy Ghost are also declined. There is no way to build a solid foundation without having the Son of God in his rightful place.

Perhaps these individuals refused Jesus because they did not believe he was the chosen Messiah that would bridge the gap between God and man. Maybe they rejected him because he was a mere carpenter who did not resemble a savior. Perhaps they declined his notions because the truth was too heavy of a weight to bear against their immortal sins. Regardless of their refusal of Jesus Christ, he is the Chief Cornerstone of our Christian formation. To be on a solid foundation, we must place him in the center, positioning us to be built up in God.

Jesus is a solid *Rock* in which our foundation is set. On one occasion, David called him the rock of his salvation, which was to say he was a strong base to stand firm (Ps 89:26). However, Jesus being the Rock is not only limited to being a foundation, but it also expands to him being the source of our strength. In the natural, rocks are multi-purposed, having unlimited functions from heating sources[6] to coating chewing gum[7]. Jesus being labeled as a rock means that he is also multi-purposeful. Scientifically, rocks are not a source of water, yet God could provide water from an unlikely source. Paul explained to believers that God provided water through Moses,

---

5. "The Little Known," lines 16–18.
6. Soelaiman, "Geothermal energy," 1–7.
7. "Are There,: lines 26–30.

but now another Rock comes to provide living water through Jesus Christ (1 Cor 10: 4). Jesus Christ is the rock in which our every need can be met as we can stand firm in him and find a never-ending well of strength.

Jesus is the well of *Living Water*, which was first mentioned within the old testament. Zechariah prophesied that out of the house of David, a fountain should rise to cleanse Jerusalem from their sins and uncleanliness (Zech 13:1). Confirmation of this Scripture occurred as our sins were washed away, and we were made clean because of our Lord and Savior Jesus Christ (Heb 10:10-12). Within our natural bodies, we use water to cleanse and hydrate. However, water also helps remove bodily waste within our digestive systems. Jesus is the living water that will cleanse us from all unrighteousness. He will be a river in our dry places and remove all sin that constipates us, or in other words, blocks us from going in the right direction (John 7:38).

Streams of living water exist in believers to help quench the wickedness that hinders our lives. Without God, we thirst after the pleasures of this world, becoming intoxicated with its nature. We fill our cups to the brim and continuously partake of this bitter water, hoping to satisfy our thirst in life. Yet it does not; so, we continually drink until we start inducing self-inflicted waterboarding. We start drowning in wickedness within this state because we seek something that will fulfill our lives' emptiness. Sin is a temporary fix. However, Jesus gives a solution to corruption by asking willing partakers to drink of him and never thirst again (John 4:13-15).

Spiritual dehydration should cease to exist due to the endless rivers God provides (John 7:38). Dehydration sets in when we are either ill, too busy, or simply forget to drink water. Within the spirit, believers can suffer from these ailments as we often become plagued by this world's cares. Like a virus, life happens, causing believers to become too busy to attend church, too busy to pray, and too busy to say, "thank you." Sooner or later, our minds are directed more towards carnal things than those that should take priority in our lives. We forget or refuse to drink from the never-ending well, causing spiritual dehydration.

Tapping into this endless source of water will cleanse us from all unrighteousness and provide spiritual nutrients. As the *Chief Shepherd*, he will not allow his sheep to fall victim to dehydration or spiritual starvation. Our God is a supplier of all our needs through the blessings of the good shepherd, Jesus Christ (Phil 4:19). David made the analogy of the Lord being like a shepherd who leads his sheep to green pastures and calming waters

(Ps 23:1–2). The shepherd's primary duty is to ensure that the flocks' needs are supplied and protect them from unseen dangers.

As our good shepherd, the Lord is also a faithful protector, who will keep us from our adversary (2 Thess 3:3). All we must do is follow his staff, and that staff is the Word of God. On one occasion, Jesus gave a parable concerning a sower who plants seeds in which birds took some; the others fell on rocks, and some among thorny ground (Matt 3:9). As a good shepherd, the Lord sows the seeds by being the Word. Yet some believers will hear this doctrine, but the adversary is quick to snatch it from their hearts. Some will joyfully hear the gospel, but in time will be tempted to go back in sin, while others will be choked by the cares of this life (Luke 8:5–15). These are all tricks of the roaring lion who wants to steer us away from the flock. However, our good shepherd always comes back for his sheep, and he leaves none behind. Alone against our adversary, we are like sheep to the slaughter, but due to his undying love, nothing can make him turn away from his flock (Rom 8:36–39).

We are precious to the Lord, and he cares about our wants, desires, and fears. One example of this is when the disciples traveled to Gadarenes and encountered a vicious storm in which they would have capsized. Frightened, they called on Jesus, saying, "Master, master, we perish" (Luke 8:24). With a few words, the sea and the wind obeyed him because he is indeed the ruler of all things. Jesus being our master, is not equivalent to someone owning slaves or servants. However, we freely choose to submit to his will. He paid for us through his blood, and now we are his servants, by choice. Unlike slaves, this is our preference as by his death; we were freed from the sin of slavery. Albeit, we have two options. We can choose for Satan to be our master, which is guaranteed death, or we can choose life by serving God.

Our servitude to Jesus Christ provides us with several benefits because he is the *head over all things* (Eph 1:22) and the *heir of all things* (Heb 1:2). This was the reward Jesus received because of his willingness to die to redeem man. God restored his rightful place in him by giving Jesus rule over all things within heaven as well as earth (Matt 28:18–20). Authority was given to Jesus to give eternal life, and with that comes our benefits (John 17:2). Granted, we did not deserve life, but because of the love God had for his creation, he gave the light of the world to the darkness of death for his sons and daughters to have life. God gave one life to save many, but that life was more significant than any life imaginable. Our lives do not amount to the life that Jesus lived for thirty-three years on Earth, yet we are joint-heirs with him because we accepted the Son.

It's not difficult to fathom that Jesus has inherited the heavens and the earth. After all, he deserved it because he is the rightful heir to the Kingdom of God. Before becoming the "God-man" called Jesus, this authority was already granted to him (John 1:1–3). Once the spirit became flesh, this power was merely transferred over to the Son of man. Authorized by his Father, Jesus has authority over life and death (Luke 7:11–15; John 11:43–44), demonic spirits (Matt 12:28–29), sickness (Luke 22:50–51), nature (Mark 11:12–14), and every living thing (Mark 11:2, John 1:3–4). As joint-heirs to Jesus Christ, this authority and power shifts to the sons and daughters of God. We do not have to wait until the thousand-year reign. However, if we are filled with the Holy Spirit, we have this authority now.

The Word of God has already provided a drafted transcript of the authority we have through Jesus Christ as he is the *Author and Perfecter of our Faith* (Heb 5:9; 5:12). Within this sense, the word *author* means the "originator or creator of something," concluding that our Christian journey starts with faith in him. Jesus himself said, "no man comes to the Father except through me" (John 14:6). Salvation begins by having faith that Jesus is God incarnate who died on the cross for our sins (Acts 16:30–31). Granted, believing this takes faith as some do not believe that Jesus lived on this earth as the Son of God. Therefore, without accepting Jesus and believing in his sovereign power, our faith is hopeless.

Increased faith happens when we begin to trust God fully. Faith is the act of hoping without necessarily seeing (Heb 11:1). Trust does not occur overnight; however, it is a process that he perfects in us. Naturally, Christians would not follow Jesus unless he provided truth in his Word. It is one thing to say that he can heal, but it would be as empty as other religious doctrines without proof of his divine healing. Therefore, the perfecting of our faith is based upon the hope that if he has healed others, then he can heal us as well.

Indeed, Jesus is a *Balm in Gilead*. The Balm of Gilead was a unique perfume that had healing capabilities. As God's people were exiled in Babylon, Jeremiah wept, saying, "Is there no balm in Gilead, is there no physician there?" (Jer 8:21–22). Judah's plight was horrendous; however, Jeremiah's heartfelt question describes many people's cries today. Surely, there is a medicine for the wounded and the broken-spirited. Though, they do not believe in the healing powers of our spiritual balm. Jesus is that balm that heals all diseases (Matt 4:23). We must simply have faith that he can and will heal.

Consider the woman who dealt with a bleeding infirmity for twelve years. After Jesus healed Jairus' daughter from death, she had joined the multitude and pressed towards him to touch his garment. Undeniably, she had heard that Jesus was a healer and perhaps even witnessed the power he possessed. If the woman had not, then her faith may not have been as strong. However, because of the perfecting process God was doing in her heart, she could be healed because her faith had made her whole (Mark 5:34).

Improving our faith in him is nothing short of a divine miracle as we walk by faith and not by sight (2 Cor 5:7). We utilize this statement to demonstrate our faith walk in God. However, when Paul said this, he was discussing our mortal deaths that would bring immortal life. It was difficult for the Jews and the Gentiles to believe; however, Jesus is the *Author of Eternal Salvation* (Heb 5:9). At some point in our lives, we have been faced with our mortality and realize that we will die one day. Paul was encouraging believers to believe that there was life after death as our old bodies will decay, and new bodies will emerge. Jesus, as our eternal salvation, means that we will never have to face death again. When he went to the cross, he tasted death for us, and by this action, we have everlasting deliverance.

Obtaining eternal salvation is a beautiful gift. It is excellent to know that we are saved on this earth, yet, being kept for all eternity is great security. In the last days, we know that men will become proud and boasters of themselves, ungrateful and unholy (1 Tim 3:1–5). Even now, we face wars and rumors of wars, with natural disasters arising more so than ever before (Mark 13:7–9). Although these things are to come and are currently happening, we have an eternal refuge in God's Son, Jesus Christ. David's confidence in God was strong during the war, in which he took faith in the salvation of God (Ps 27:3–4). This does not necessarily mean that we will be exempt from these occurrences, yet we know that death is not our end. Our eternal salvation brings forth an everlasting refuge in the Almighty.

Just as David found a temporary haven in the hills, his eternal help came from God (Ps 121:1–2). Understanding that God is our help brings forth great peace of mind because we are saved in this world and the next. Jesus is the *Author of our Peace* as he originates peace within our lives. Without him, there is no peace. As Christians, we are blessed with peace as he tells us to cast all our cares on him (Ps 29:11, 1 Pet 5:7). Establishing our manifested peace means keeping our minds committed to God. Instead of looking at the problem, we must look to God. Focusing on the issue only leads to worry, fear, and doubt. God can sustain us through the storms of life, but we must trust in his ability. Keeping our eyes on God leads to peace in our lives. Jesus told his disciples their hearts should not be troubled; if they believed in God, they should also believe in him (John 14:1). Jesus has already authorized peace into our lives; it is our responsibility to pursue it (Ps 34:14).

Peace in God does not exempt us from life problems. As having a relationship with God seems to increase our challenges. Nevertheless, his peace will sustain us through our troubles to the point that it is difficult to understand our state of calm (Phil4:7). Despite going through his persecution, Apostle Paul encouraged believers on multiple occasions saying, "grace and peace come unto you" (Phil1:2, Eph 1:2, 1 Cor1:3). This greeting of peace helped Jews and Gentiles understand that despite our trials and tribulations, God will grant us unmerited favor and peace throughout life's problems.

Often our peace does not make sense; it is hard to comprehend. When we take observation of our problems, they seem too impossible to handle. The mortgage is due. College loans are in default. Children need braces. Marriage is on the brink of divorce; sudden death in the family; just been diagnosed with cancer. Naturally, our first response is to become worried, yet before our anxiety sets into full-blown panic, we need to remember that Jesus has ordained peace in our lives. The Peace of God will allow us to see those problems as steppingstones to trusting him more. Imaginably, God sits on the throne of grace, saying, "I just took your son, but will you still trust me? "You've been diagnosed with Aids, but will you still have faith in me?" God's peace will overtake us more than our problems ever will. Our responsibility is to latch on to the gift of peace and ask God to grant it to us.

Peter's prayer was that the grace and peace of God be multiplied to his believers, which means that peace should flow abundantly within our lives (2 Pet 1:2). One of the first titles Jesus was given before his birth was the *Prince of Peace* (Isa 9:6). Jesus does not just sprinkle out peace. However, he drowns us with tranquility. The Greek meaning of the word prince is captain, which means Jesus is the head of peace. As the Prince of Peace, he oversees it. One of his missions on earth was to bring peace to a corrupt world. Before his arrival, the world had abandoned God's way, resulting in chaos, confusion, and turmoil. Since God is the author of peace, he sent his

Son so our hearts would not be weary but will be full of the peace (1 Cor 14:33, John 14:27).

Restoring our relationship in God was needed to establish and maintain peace within our lives. The world's sense of serenity is different than the peace of God. We cannot trust our government as it is run by people with their own motives and agendas. God is for us, and his only plan is that we have eternal life. There is no greater peace in knowing that we are guaranteed an everlasting covenant with God after this life. However, our relationship had to be rekindled with him before we could have this promise. Manifesting peace means that we must continually pursue God for everything in our lives. Our prayer should be that the Prince of Peace continues to blanket us with his grace and peace as we continue to restore our relationship with God.

Another name Jesus was given before his birth was the *Everlasting Father* (Isa 9:6). This name brings some confusion as it indicates that Jesus is the Father, in which the Holy Trinity does not exist. This is not true. The Hebrew interpretation means "Father of Eternity" or merely the originator of everlasting life. In our culture, we use the word father to denote a person who originated something such as Alexander Graham Bell, the creator of the telephone, or the Wright Brothers of the airplane. George Washington has been deemed the Father of the United States because he was instrumental in its establishment. Therefore, Jesus' title as the Everlasting Father means that he is the originator of everlasting life, for he has the keys to eternal existence (Rev 1:18).

It is befitting that Isaiah gave Jesus, the Son of God, this title as he was part of life's creation. Within the natural, life cannot begin without the father's seed, and our Christian life cannot commence without Jesus Christ. God is the Father within the Holy Trinity; however, Jesus being the Everlasting Father validates the Scriptures that God gave his Son so we could have life eternal (John 10:28–30; 1 Pet 5:10; 1 John 5:11; John 3:16). It is clear, with no recognition of the Son, we cannot have eternal life. God, the Father, gave life to Adam, but we all must die due to sin, but when the Everlasting Father gives life, we all can obtain this life eternally (1 Cor 15:22).

During Pentecost, Peter boldly proclaimed the life and death of Jesus Christ, in which thousands were added to the Kingdom of God. The multitude had witnessed the Holy Ghost's power and understood that through Jesus, there was life after death. Even though the Sadducees saw the many signs and wonders performed, they were still indignant to the gospel because they did not believe in the resurrection (Acts 4:1–2; 23:8). Threatening Peter and John, they threw them in prison only to escape as the power of God released the doors. The renewal of their freedom was another way that the *Prince of Life* used the resurrecting power to regain their lives from pending death.

Peter's impromptu message delivered the name Prince of Life as he spoke to those at the temple (Acts 3:15). As the people witnessed the miracle of the lame man walking, Peter boldly proclaimed that this man could walk by the power and authority granted by Jesus. His sermon revealed the true nature of Christ as the overseer of life. God, the Father, gives life; however, he has given his Son this right to provide this life more abundantly (John 5:21; 10:10). Despite the death that several shall encounter, Jesus promises believers everlasting life through the power of the resurrection. By his death, death is abolished, and after our death comes life eternally (2 Tim 1:10).

Just as Jesus has been given the authority to give life, he has also been given the power to provide death (Hebrew 9:27). On the day of judgment, Jesus will separate believers from unbelievers as he has been deemed *Judge of the Living and the Dead* (Acts 10:42). During the judgment, Jesus will separate those who grudgingly rejected him from those who followed the voice of truth. Our eternal outcome depends on the final word of our Savior. It is he who holds our fate in his hands. Everyone will have to appear before the judgment seat to make an account of their humanly deeds as no one is exempted (2 Cor 5:10).

Ironically, before being judge, he is an *Advocate* in our defense (I John 2:1). As our advocate and attorney, he makes a case for our innocence. Indeed, we are guilty, but our Savior never ceases to stop pleading our case before God. Envision a courtroom where we are the accused, and Satan is our accuser. Satan has boxes upon boxes of evidence of every evil deed we committed, and the worst part is that our prosecutor is correct. Satan stands before God prepared to make his case for our eternal damnation, and we peer over to the defense table in which Jesus looks unprepared. There are no boxes of evidence of our good works, no character witnesses, not even a recommendation letter on our behalf. As Satan begins to make an account of our sins, he rests his case. Then Jesus steps up before God, shows him the nail prints in his hands, and smears his blood over Satan's evidence, and we are found not guilty. He is the *Wonderful Counselor* because he never lost a case.

Jesus Christ, The Savior

Amazingly, this title is not just limited to Jesus being our great intercessor, however during biblical times, the word counselor meant a wise ruler or adviser. Often, people would seek the wisdom of a counselor concerning governmental or personal affairs. First Chronicles 27:32 referred to Jonathan as a counselor because he was a man of understanding. Proverbs discussed how a wise man would seek many counselors and become victorious (Prov 11:14, 12:15, and 24:6). It is good that we can seek Godly advice from our church leaders. However, we have a King that surpasses all others. God said if any man lacks wisdom, they can ask for it, and he will freely give it unto them (Jas1:5). Jesus is full of knowledge and truth and will guide us in the right direction if we listen to his voice.

Remember the adulterous woman who was brought before Jesus (John 8:1-11). Even though she was not seeking wisdom, she found it. At this moment, our Savior demonstrated his wisdom to save her natural and spiritual life. The Pharisees thought they could outmaneuver Jesus' logic by forcing him to judge a sinner publicly. However, instead of condemning the woman, Jesus overturned it, causing the men to examine their own lives. God's wisdom is parallel to none. In this instance, he established his wisdom by outwitting those who thought they were cleverer than him.

As our *Teacher*, his life instructs believers on how we should walk before God daily. One of the paramount illustrations of this journey was demonstrated through Jesus putting the Father first. Throughout his life, Jesus never boasted of himself but always gave glory to God. He could have quickly received praises as they both are one but gave it to God. On one occasion, he admits that his Father is greater than him (John 14:28). This statement seemed contradictory as both are equal within the Holy Trinity. Still, Jesus understood that he was less than God because he was now the Son of Man, made into flesh. Therefore, through Jesus' example, we realize we must first give glory to God as he is the one that sustains our being.

Another teaching from Jesus was the lesson on how to love as he loved (Eph 5:1-2). Since love is one of God's essential characteristics, we must also demonstrate this character trait within our lives (I John 4:7-8). There are several examples of love found within the Bible; however, none are equivalent to God's love for his creation (John 3:16). He loved us so much that he gave his Son to die so we could live (John 15:13). Through this example, Christ demonstrated the agape love that Paul emphasized within First Corinthians chapter 13. "Love is patient and kind; love does not envy or boast; it is not arrogant or rude. It does not rejoice at wrongdoing but rejoices with the truth. Love bears all things, believes all things, hopes all things, endures all things. Love never ends (verses 4–8)". God's love for us continues for all eternity, therefore through Christ, he gave instructions to love each other (Matt 22: 39; 1 Pet 2:17), how to love our enemies (Matt 5:44), our spouses (Eph 5:25), and most of all how to love God (Matt 22:37).

The love of God also teaches us how to endure hardship. Jesus provided this example during the period of his death. The humility that our Lord and Savior faced was unbefitting for his status as they mockingly clothed him in purple, placing a crown of thorns on his head. They tortured him while hailing him as the *King of the Jews* (Mark 15:18) and the *King of Israel* (Mark 15:32), not knowing that their acts of cruelty were merely a part of God's plan. We must also see our suffering as the will of God. Our hardships are for a short period, but once they are finished, we are restored, confirmed, strengthened, and established (1 Pet 5:10). Therefore, we should rejoice in our suffering as it brings forth a more remarkable outcome (Rom 5:3–4). If Jesus did not endure the cross, he still would have been King, but the greater result was that we all could inherit eternal life.

Another lesson Jesus demonstrated was humility during the last supper. Jesus humbled himself to wash his disciples' feet and established how believers should act by this simple performance. Journeys often occurred by walking, and it was customary that before entering someone's home, their feet had to be washed. As our Teacher, he taught his followers how to have humility, take care of one another, and be thoughtful. Some churches still participate in this ritual. However, the actual feet washing is continued acts of self-effacement, kindness, and love. By demonstrating these traits, we will be able to enter into his heavenly home.

Jesus took on a servant's role and was made into a man's likeness to instruct us on how to live (Phil2:5–8). By doing this, Jesus taught us how to serve others as he continues to serve all creation. Our discipleship is based upon the foundation of servanthood. Jesus Christ came to earth to fulfill his Father's will (John 6:38). This example demonstrates that we also are here to serve the will of God. The perfect will of our Father is to love him and to love others. If we do this, then we are servants of God. Jesus's servant's heart showed his greatness as a dedicated teacher. The world's system believes that the served is greater. However, our Savior understood that the one who serves is superior (Luke 22:27). Our servitude to Christ allows us to take on a relationship that calls us to be better than what we thought we could ever be.

Jesus Christ, The Savior

Jesus taught his disciples many servitude lessons, which earned him the title *Rabbi*, meaning teacher or master[8]. Even Nicodemus, a historian, called Jesus by this title understood his role as a well-informed teacher sent by God (John 3:1–2). In modern-day Judaism, this name has advanced to a more formal designation as a person who studies that religion. However, this name was less informal during biblical times as John the Baptist and others were called rabbi because of their excellent knowledge.

Jesus warned against calling others, mainly the Pharisees, rabbi not because they lacked wisdom, but because of their hypocrisy. As leaders of the church, individuals must be careful not to become self-righteous, understanding that there is only one *Holy and Righteous One*: Jesus Christ. After Peter healed the lame man, he immediately gave our Savior credit (Acts 3:11–14). Peter understood he was there to aid in the healing, but the manifested power came from God. The *Holy One of God* is set apart from even those who are holy. Immorality has happened to every man except Jesus Christ; therefore, he is deemed Holy of the holies. Our righteousness only happens because of Christ (2 Cor 5:21). It is ill-advised to think we are morally superior when there was only one who withstood sin. Our *Great High Priest* went through every temptation and did not yield (Heb 4:15). Since every human has surrendered to evil at least once in their lives, how can we think of ourselves as self-righteous when there is only one who weathered sin, and that is our great priest, Jesus Christ.

During the old testament, the high priest was elected from the tribe of Levi "to act on the behalf of men in relation to God, to offer gifts, and sacrifices for sins" (Heb 5:10). One of the most critical roles of this position occurred during The Day of Atonement. The high priest was to conduct the sacrificial ceremony, which reconciled God's people's relationship with him. As Melchizedek was the first priest, Jesus became the last who acted on our behalf by offering his life as an eternal gift and became the sacrificial lamb for our sins (Heb 7:1). He is a High Priest who is "holy, harmless, undefiled, separate from sinners, and made higher than the heavens" (Heb 7:26). Under the Jewish law, men appointed high priests, but thankfully our High Priest was appointed by God, who will reign forever (verse 28).

God selected a faithful High Priest and *Apostle* within his Son, Jesus Christ (Heb 3:1). We often do not refer to Jesus as an apostle, as the The Apostles' Creed is based upon his life and death[9]. However, this title's

---

8. "Rabbi," line 1.
9. Wilson, "What is," lines 1–5.

definition suggests a person who is sent to train others about the Word of God. Jesus appears to have been the original Apostle, as God sent him to redeem, and Jesus then instructed the disciples to train others within the gospel. Jesus was indeed "sent out as a messenger" to do his Father's will as he was equipped with a specific mission to teach and preach salvation to the world. When he accepted the call to redeem man, he inversely accepted the call to become an apostle.

Assuming this role seems similar to ancient Jewish marriage customs as God arranged for Jesus to take us as his bride. His apostleship caused him to be sent out like the groom is sent out to retrieve his spouse. Most marriages were arranged by the fathers, in which the groom's family "purchased" the bride. Both the father of the bride and the groom would sign the "ketubah" or marriage contract[10]. The couple's betrothal or engagement was a binding agreement with all the marriage rights except for cohabitation and consumption. The groom would then leave to set up a bridal chamber in his father's home. The length of time was unknown and would generally be announced by a trumpet to prepare the bride. Once the announcement was made, the bride would be presented to the groom and taken home.

During his ministry, Jesus often used the analogy of marriage to demonstrate his apostleship here on earth. God, the Father, sent his Son Jesus Christ as the *Bridegroom* of the church. To seal the contract, he purchased us with his divine blood to cleanse us from our sins (Acts 20:28). Our engagement with Jesus should be binding, meaning that our commitment to him should be unwavering as we wait for his return. Just like the groom who went to prepare the bridal chamber for his bride, Jesus prepares a place for us (John 14:3). We do not know when our bridegroom will return. However, when we hear the trumpet sound, we will know that he has come to take us home (1 Thess 4:16–17).

Another name given to Jesus is the *Rose of Sharon* or the *Lily of the Valley*, which originated as a name for one of King Solomon's wives (Songs of Solomon 2:1). Within the book of Songs, we learn of King Solomon's love and admiration for his beloved. However, ironically, there is nowhere in the Bible that Jesus is referred to by these names. If this is the case, then how did these names initiate to the Son of God.

The Songs of Solomon is a collection of writings that demonstrate the feelings between Solomon and his bride. Many have wondered why this

---

10. Lamm, "The Jewish," lines 1–4.

book is among the others within the Bible. The simple answer is that this book exhibits the strong passion Solomon had for his beloved, yet it is incomprehensible to God's love for us. The symbolism of the Rose of Sharon and the Lily of the Valley can be linked to King Solomon's bride and the Bridegroom Jesus Christ as both have been deemed beautiful. Solomon's bride referring to herself like the rose of Sharon, indicates her confidence in her beauty since the rose, symbolically, is known as one of the most stunning flowers worldwide. Ironically, metaphorically saying that Jesus is the Rose of Sharon suggests that he is overall beautiful, not only in physical attractiveness but within. The lily indication shows the purity and humility of Jesus Christ, who was without sin, yet humbled himself to the cross. Despite this name not being mentioned in the Bible for Jesus, it distinguishes his beauty, pureness, and humility as the Son of God.

Regardless of Solomon's reputation of having several wives, he still understood the loveliness of this one wife. Jesus as the Rose of Sharon and Lily of the Valley demonstrates that divine beauty. With the billions of people in the world and the decillion that have died over time, Jesus saw each one of God's Children. When we think of all the people in the world, it is hard to comprehend that he died explicitly for us. However, just as Solomon distinguished this one wife, Jesus exclusively distinguished us as his bride. The uniqueness of Jesus' love is incomprehensible as, despite the many, he saw only one. We must take his death personal as he died for the world, but our individualized relationships with him makes it unique.

A verse in Song of Solomon says, "My beloved is mine, and I am his" (2:16). Even though Solomon's wife was referring to her husband, Jesus is our beloved Savior despite our acceptance of him or not. For sure, we are his, as we are "the flock he pastures among the lilies." Despite our flaws, his love for us surpasses any human affection that we can ever have for one another. We do not deserve this unconditional love, yet he gives it to us freely. Hell is what we should experience, but our Savior's undying love rescues us from the fiery pit.

Our debt of sin could never be paid. No matter how many acts of gratitude that we could offer or how many works we could attempt to give, we could never do enough to match the sins we committed against God. Even one sin is too much as God is holy and cannot even stand the sight of sin (Hab 1:13). Sin is a powerful force that separates us from the love of God. Our transgressions served as a large gap between the Father and his Creation.

Nevertheless, God arranged a divine bridge that would connect us back to him within his Son, Jesus Christ. As our Savior, our Lord redeemed us from our adversary to restore us to the Father. He was sent on the ultimate rescue mission to save a world from sin. Through his death, we are healed, delivered, and set free. We can live because our Savior died.

Chapter 8

THE REVELATION NAMES OF JESUS CHRIST

I am Alpha and Omega, the beginning and the ending, saith the Lord, which is, and which was, and which is to come, the Almighty.

REVELATION 1:8

HIS FIRST NIGHT ON earth was in an animal's barn, sleeping in a makeshift crib. Even before entering into this world, it appeared that no one had room for his arrival. This ultimately foreshadowed his entire thirty-three years of life. His mother and his father, a simple carpenter, brought forth a child that grew not only in stature but in humility. This child was subjected to his earthly parents and the government's laws despite earlier prophecies that "the government would be on his shoulders." When he became an adult, he was persecuted by those who vowed to keep God's law, but did not recognize the resemblance between him and his Father. Even his death was humiliating as he hung naked before men. Suffering the most agonizing death possible, that the weight of his own body caused asphyxiation. It seems that he was a simple man who, with meekness, entered the world and died within it. However, by his death and resurrection, his majesty was restored, becoming the *firstborn of the dead*, ultimately unmasking the mysteries of the Second Coming of the eternal King, Jesus Christ.

The book of Revelation is notably called the Revelation of Jesus Christ. It uses apocalyptic prophecies to unveil this ordinary man's secrecy who came from humble beginnings to become the eternal king. One of the most exciting items concerning this book is the definition of the word revelation, which means "a surprising and previously unknown fact, especially one that is made known in a dramatic way." Scholars of Revelation understand this to be one of the most theatrical books within the Bible as it unveils the mysteries of Jesus Christ, to a world that genuinely did not know him.

One of the first names given to Jesus is the *firstborn from the dead* (Rev 1:5) and the *firstborn of all creation* (Col 1:15). John used the Greek term *prototokos* meaning firstborn or first[1], to establish Jesus having complete rule over both life and death (Col 2:10). The name the firstborn from the dead appears to be the definition of an oxymoron, as anything dead cannot become alive.

Before Jesus, some resurrections occurred within the old testament as both Elisha and Elijah raised Zarephath and Shunammite's sons (1 Kgs 17:17–24; 2 Kgs 4:20–37). Additionally, in the new testament, Jesus raised Jairus' daughter and Lazarus (Mark 5:35–43; John 11:1–44). Yet, in Revelation, we find that Jesus is named the firstborn of the dead even though several other noted resurrections occurred during biblical times (2 Kgs 13:21; Acts 9:36–41; & Acts 20:7–12).

Jesus is recognized as the firstborn of the dead because each individual raised from the dead experienced death again. However, Jesus was the first one to die and live. After Calvary, he rose again and lived on the earth for an additional forty days before going back to heaven (Acts 1:3). During this time, he appeared to the disciples strengthening their faith concerning his previous teachings of life after death (1 Cor 15:6). Ascending back to heaven, Jesus was able to fully demonstrate that he was the firstborn of the dead as many saw him crucified and then resurrected, never to encounter death once again.

After his death, he reclaimed his title as the head of the church (Col 1:8). Customarily, within the old testament, the firstborn son inherited their father's role as head of the family. As the firstborn of all creation, he gained his inheritance from our heavenly Father, which granted him power and dominion. However, being the firstborn of the dead gave him control over life and death (Eph 1:21; Phil2:9). All authority was granted to him through his resurrection, thus fulfilling Abraham and God's covenant, which seemed to be lost during his years on earth, but now fully restored (Gal 3:16).

---

1. White, "Prototokos," lines 8–11.

The Revelation Names of Jesus Christ

Since Jesus is the first of creation and the firstborn of the dead, he refers to himself as *Alpha* and *Omega, the Beginning* and *the End*, and the *First* and *the Last* (Rev 1:8; 22:13-21). These three titles suggest that he pre-existed before time and will remain hereafter. Alpha and Omega are the first and last letters within the Greek Alphabet, indicating that Jesus is the first and the last. We understand this to be accurate as the first book of the Bible gives us insight into Jesus being the first in creation. As God formed man, he talks with his Son saying, "let us make man in our image." This pronoun indicates that God was conversing with another holy being before the creation of Adam. Since the first man was Adam, there had to be another deity that possessed the same image as our heavenly Father. Colossians 1:15-17 confirms this as Jesus is not only equal to God, but he is God. Thus, concluding that God was speaking to his Son, Jesus Christ.

Theologians often support this theory by mentioning the first chapter of John, which declares that Jesus was also in the beginning as the *Word* or *Logos*. The term Logos is a Greek term meaning word, principle, or thought[2]. Jesus, being referred to as the Logos, can indicate that he was the principle and God's standard. Therefore, the first verse can be translated to Jesus having the same mindset of God and that his standard was established before the foundation of time. Jesus as the Word also specifies that he and God are the same, henceforth together in the beginning when creation was formed (John 10:30).

The name the *Word of God* also appears in the book of Revelation. Ironically, this book is the last within the Bible that acknowledges that Christ was, is, and is to come (Rev 4:8). John, who also identified that the Word was in the beginning, also foretold the victory of Christ, in the end, showing forth that he is both Alpha and Omega. It was befitting for John to call Jesus The Word of God as he appears to be the only person who saw Jesus in life, death, resurrected, and then divinely restored. John's proclamation that Jesus was in the beginning as the Word resembled the same decree that he shall be in the end. Even though we could not witness Jesus's life like John, the Word of God is still alive and active today. No man has seen God, but through his Word, He is revealed, speaks as God, and is recognized as God (John 1:18).

Within the Old Testament, Jesus did not walk in the flesh but was sent as the Word to accomplish God's divine will (Isa 55:11). On several occasions, the Word of God was sent, causing several extraordinary events to

---

2. "Logos," lines 1-3.

occur. When God sent his words to Abraham, he left his country to become the father of many nations (Gen 12:1–3). Noah heard the Word of God and was able to build an arc to save his family from the great flood (Gen 6:8–22). The Israelites were delivered from captivity for over four hundred years when God spoke to Moses (Exod 4:30). Likewise, when Joshua heard the word of God, the priests were able to carry the ark of the covenant across the Jordan river, ultimately defeating Jericho (Josh 3:9; 6:16). The Word of God spoke, and incredible life-altering changes occurred. Even though we do not have Jesus in the flesh, we have the Word of God.

From eternity to eternity, John established that the Word was in the beginning and within the end. Only by the Word was the world fashion, and only by his Words are we able to live in him, die in him, and be raised from the dead because of him. Never within existence was the Word of God not present as Matthew 24:35 reminds us that heaven and earth shall pass away, but the Word of God will always remain. In John's vision, he saw the Word covered in a blood-drenched robe descending from heaven on a white horse, surrounded by the armies of heaven (Rev 19:11–14). To Christians, this encounter is known as the Second Coming of Jesus Christ. When the Word of God comes back to reclaim his throne, establishing that he is the beginning and the end.

Envision this ordinary man, that was called the *Lamb of God*, who made himself of no reputation, returning to overcome the sins of the world. The analogy of Jesus being a lamb represents his unadulterated nature, such as the lambs chosen during the Passover. Within ancient Israel, the lamb was symbolic of purity and cleanliness. Lamb selection was crucial as God gave clear instructions on choosing this animal. One of the main requirements was that the lamb had to have no faults or defects. Unblemished by sin, he elected himself to become the sacrificial lamb similarly to the lambs chosen to deliver the Israelites from Egypt. The blood placed on the doorpost was simply a foreshadowing of the divine blood that would later cover our sins, passing over death to inherit everlasting life.

To understand the comparison between Jesus as the Lamb of God, we must uncover the position of sin and the sin offering. When sin entered the world, Adam and Eve realized they were naked before God attempting to cover their shame. Ironically, we also make a poor effort to mask our sins with artificial layers of good works and deeds. However, nothing conceals the ugliness of sin but blood, which requires death.

Sin leaves us exposed before God, naked and afraid. Therefore, God made them garments of skins to cover their shame. Even though the Bible does not mention using animal skins, we can make this inference as there were only two humans in the world. Indeed, God didn't provide synthetic skins as Adam and Eve wouldn't have learned the burdensome cost of sin. Remember, death did not enter the world until sin superseded it, indicating that death would have been nonexistent if there was no sin (Rom 5:12). Therefore, to atone for their sins, death had to occur so they might live.

The causal impact of sin equates to death; for one to live, something must die. Life comes from the blood, and without this fluid, there is no life. To prevent impending death, God provided animals' blood to atone for Israel's sins within the Old Testament (Lev 17:11). Specific animals were used according to the person's status or wealth to make amends for their iniquities. The offender would place their hands over the innocent animal during the sin offering, feeling the life drain from its body. The blood would then be sprinkled on the veil and smeared on the horns of the altar. The remaining blood would be poured at the foot of the table while the remains were discarded, ultimately demonstrating the waste of sin.

Impractically, not utilizing these items appears to be an analogy of the sinful life useless to God. Animals were a commodity that provided a source of survival for the Israelites. No one, wealthy or poor, had the luxury of killing them without fully taking advantage of the parts that remained. Daily and annually, animals were slaughtered to atone for sin, resulting in millions of innocent animals being killed without complete use. Again, proving that a sinful life cannot fulfill God's purpose unless the life-giving blood reconciles it.

The animal sacrifice was the perfect law of God given to imperfect people as it served as an atonement of sin. This act was done as repentance to God; however, the animals' blood was not enough to remove sin. Consequentially, this is why the sin offering had to be done frequently as the Israelites were still connected to their iniquities. As his ways are always perfect, God had another solution for atonement. Ultimately detaching believers from sin and death would provide the last slaughtering of the innocent in his Son, Jesus Christ. Through the death of the Lamb of God, we are no longer connected to death as his divine blood covers our sins and faults.

In Revelation, chapter 5, John reveals a book with seven seals that no man is found worthy to open. The gospel's commentariats have referenced this scroll as the same one witnessed by Daniel (Dan 12:4-9). The Lord revealed to Daniel that the mysteries of its content would not be disclosed until the end of time. In Revelation 5:5, we learn that the slain Lamb, who has redeemed us by his blood, is worthy to open the book. When each seal is released, more revelations of judgment are revealed (Rev 6–9), and those who survive will seek death as they fear the wrath of the Lamb (Rev 6:16)

The *Lion of Judah*, the *Root of David*, was the only one found worthy to break the seals. The Lion of Judah refers to the blessings Jacob gave his son Judah on his deathbed. Despite Judah's past faults, he was blessed among his brothers and was chosen to be part of Jesus Christ's genealogy. Jacob referred to his son as a *lion's whelp* or cub due to his fearlessness and courageousness. Within the blessing, Jacob also states that "the scepter shall not depart from him," demonstrating the everlasting rule Judah's descendants will have over Israel. King David also came from this tribe, notably distinguishing Jesus as the root of David.

A corresponding prophecy is also seen in Numbers 24:17, which states, "there shall come a Star out of Jacob, and the Scepter shall rise out of Israel." We see this being fulfilled in Rev 22:16 as Jesus identifies himself as the "*Bright and Morning Star.*" Ironically, this name parallels with Satan's name, Lucifer, which is Latin for the planet Venus as the "morning star"[3] (Isa 14:12–14, Luke 10:18). Before his fall, Satan was the brightest among all the angels as Venus was one of the brightest "stars" within the galaxy. Even though both Jesus and our adversary share this title, the Son of God is described as the *bright* morning star distinguishing from the two. Since the creation cannot be greater than the creator, the adjective bright sets Jesus apart as the world's leading light.

Coincidently, this is not the only name shared between Jesus and Satan as both have been described as lions (Rev 5:5; 1 Pet 5:8). Again, each is equally different as Satan is disproportionate to the royal statue of Judah's Lion. Peter describes Satan as a roaring lion devouring whomever he seeks, yet Jesus is the direct opposite as he saves those he encounters (1 Pet 5:8). Due to their status, the lion's symbol often represents leadership, royalty, and strength, which is contradictory to Satan's standing. These animals also are known as savage predators, which is causally related to his character but contradictory to Jesus's.

However, in Revelation 6:16, Jesus is described as a wrathful lamb, which appears to be an oxymoron as rage is a character trait of the lion versus the gentle and meekness of a baby sheep. The Bible implies that the

---

3. "Lucifer," lines 1–7.

Lamb of God, who was once subdued to the cross, will take on characteristics of a ferocious lion ready for battle, preparing for judgment. While Jesus was on earth, we rarely see him exhibiting characteristics of a strong man. However, Jesus possessed a quiet strength like a sleeping lion. In the wild, lions do not attack unless they are provoked. They typically lie dormant until the time comes to show forth their strength. Our Lord and Savior's character is of that lion who lies waiting for the moment to unleash his judgment upon the world.

With the breaking of each seal, the world will face venomous condemnation. Breaking of the first four seals will release four horsemen that will bring forth plagues, war, famine, and substantial death (Rev 6:1–8). The martyrs' cries will begin after the next seal is broken, in which catastrophic natural disasters will occur, and all the earthly light sources will cease to exist (Rev 6:9–17). Finally, the seventh seal will reveal the seven angels waiting to blow their trumpets, bringing forth other disasters and killing one-third of the world's population (Rev 8–9). At the seventh trumpet, the "mysteries of God will be fulfilled," in which He will redeem his kingdom confirming the Lord's prayer "your kingdom come, your will be done" (Matt 4:8) as well as fulfilling Daniel's earlier prophecies (Dan 2:44; 7:14).

Within his vision, Daniel saw four beasts, three of which represented world powers; yet the fourth beast differed by its exceeding strength with ten horns (Dan 7:7). John also saw four beasts that had similar characteristics to the ones witnessed by Daniel. Theologians have often disputed that these beasts differ, while others believe they are the same. Nevertheless, we know that these beasts depict events of the last days. Within both images, there was a beast with ten horns. Each crown represented ten kings that will oppose the law of God, giving their kingdoms to the beast (Rev 13). John speaks of these beings as the antichrist, both in the singular and plural sense, as there is one central evil that has control over many (I John 2:18–25). Symbolically, the three beasts represent Satan, the antichrist, and the false prophet. Between them, an unholy trinity will rise that will perform miracles and unite the ten kings and kingdoms of the world to war against the Lamb of God (Rev 16:13–14). Nevertheless, Daniel also saw God, the *Ancient of days*, sitting upon the throne, and he observed the *Son of man* descend from heaven restoring his everlasting kingdom.

People have considered why God is called the Ancient of days, and Jesus is called the Son of man. In reviewing the term ancient, it often refers to something old, and as a noun, it exhibits an older person. Theologians have pondered why Daniel described God in this manner, and many have speculated that it showcases God's continual existence. In the beginning, God made the heavens and earth, and then he created light to distinguish night from day. However, days did not exist before this, showing that God existed before forming days, indicating the Almighty God's agelessness.

Jesus being the Son of man, meant he was both human as well as divine. On several occasions, he referred to himself as the Son of man to show his humility versus his divinity. Quickly Jesus could have proclaimed to be the Son of God and commanded all to follow him, yet with unpretentiousness, Jesus humbled himself as a servant instead of a god (Matt 20:28). When Daniel proclaimed to see the Son of man, he did not know Jesus, yet he saw an individual surrounded by the glory which could be deemed a god but looked like an average human. Daniel's vision also corresponded with Zechariah's prophecy that Jesus would be the *Horn of Salvation* (Luke 1:69), which would ultimately destroy the horns that make war against the Lamb of God. This horn of salvation will destroy the evil systems of this world to restore his kingdom.

Christ was given the name *Prince of the kings of the earth*, incontrovertibly establishing that all authority is given to him by the Father. However, we must understand the origins of his supremacy throughout the world as ten kings will reign over their kingdoms. An important fact to note is that these kings are not actual monarchs; however, they are government officials such as presidents, chancellors, or prime ministers. These heads of the government will unite to form a one-world order by denouncing their authority. Unification often brings forth great strength, and these administrations will dominate as one force causing several to take on the symbol of the beast.

Another beast having two horns like a lamb but speaking like a dragon will unite the earth's inhabitants to become devoted to this central world order. Posing as a messiah, he will perform wonders that are only known to God. Ironically, the miracle of fire, which caused many people to believe during Elijah's time (1 Kgs 18:38), will ultimately cause many people to doubt in the end days. Undisputedly, this world system will be significantly esteemed as the highest official on earth deceiving many (Rev 13).

For three and a half years, the antichrist will reign to set up his kingdom and then persecute the church for an additional period (Rev 13:5). The beast will appear to have complete control over the earth and its inhabitants. At which time, he will gain sole authority over legislation, commercial, judicial, and executive divisions. He will exalt and magnify himself above every other head of state (Dan 11:36) while believing that he is god (2 Thess 2:4). Misled by the miracles and his call for world peace, he will deceive and destroy billions who remain on the earth (Dan 8:23–25). Even within our time with cruel rulers such as Adolf Hitler, Mao Zedong, Pol Pot, and Idi Amin, the antichrist's influence will surpass them all, gaining more power than any government official throughout historical existence.

These men's cruelty collectively killed over twelve million people, yet the antichrist will exceed this number, dooming all who follow him to everlasting death. Currently, over seven billion people are living on earth, and growing numbers each year. Even if that number is 1 percent of the world's population, millions upon millions of people will suffer eternal death at the kingship of the antichrist.

Paul quoted Isaiah stating that Abraham's descendants would outnumber the sand, but only a portion would be steadfast (Rom 9:27). In Revelation 7:3–8, 144,000 individuals from the twelve tribes of Israel will have the seal of God to be saved. This small remnant will be known as the tribulation saints. Satan will continue to war against those who believe in God, yet this small group shall keep the testimony of Jesus Christ to be delivered from the hands of the enemy (Rev 12:17).

This testimony is merely a prophecy concerning Jesus' authority within heaven and earth (Rev 19:10). Despite the new world order that is to come, Jesus will continue to have full power (Matt 28:18). Peter gave an account of God's influence on the day of Pentecost, affirming that it was not by Roman's control Jesus was put to death, but by the power of God, which caused him to be also raised from the dead (Acts 2:23–24). While on trial, he told Pilate that he had no power to crucify or release him, but all power came from above (John 19:11). Jesus' authority was never granted as his Father merely gave it. However, once he became human, this power had to be reestablished through his death, which was the almighty plan of God.

Messianic prophecies were told by Isaiah proclaiming that a child would be born, and the government would be upon his shoulders. This foretold the weight Jesus would carry as the official prince of the kings of the earth. Consequently, this coincided with Jacob's blessing that "the scepter would not depart from Judah, nor a lawgiver from between his feet, until Shiloh come; and unto him shall the gathering of the people be" (Gen 49:10). Inside these prophetic words, we see that there will always be a royal lineage or ruling government in Judah's bloodline until Shiloh comes.

Arguments have resulted from this ambiguous phrase, as some believed it referenced the biblical city in which the ark of the covenant remained. In contrast, others think that it referenced a biblical figure. The name Shiloh was used in the Jewish encyclopedia, the Talmud, as a name for the Messiah. Others render the name to mean "one who is sent out," "the peaceful one," or the "rest-giver," which also links Isaiah's prophecy with Jesus, being the *Prince of Peace* (Isa 9:6). Therefore, it is believed that Jacob's blessings to Judah was an everlasting covenant until Jesus' reign when peace comes.

The next phase of Jacob's blessings, "unto him shall the gathering of the people be," appears to reference Psalm 50. Asaph, the writer of this chapter, discussed the mighty God who will one day assemble all the people for judgment, which we know happens at the end of days. Corresponding with the Second Coming of Jesus Christ, Asaph also writes about the judgment that John saw within his vision. Asaph states, "Our God comes and will not be silent; a fire devours before him and around him a tempest rages" (Ps 50:4 NIV). John witnessed the great lake of fire where the satanic trinity will be devoured in torment forever. Not only this, but he also saw the gathering of the dead for the day of judgment (Rev 20:9–15). Both prophecies demonstrate the biblical truths concerning God's judgment in which no one, dead or alive, will be able to escape.

During the Battle of Armageddon, as the ten kings continued war against the people of God, John saw Jesus, the *Faithful and True* one, descending from heaven. A name was written that no one knew, and on his thigh was written, KING OF KINGS AND LORD OF LORDS (Rev 19:11–16). He prepares himself for victory in the heat of battle, followed by heaven's armies to overthrow the beast and reclaim his throne. To understand these three names' significance, it is vital to understand their origins and implications of triumph within the last days.

As we see at the end of Revelation, Jesus was also called the *Faithful and True Witness* and the *Faithful Witness* at the beginning of this book (Rev 1:5, Rev 3:14). The word witness is a noun with two meanings: "a person who sees an event" and "evidence or proof." Jesus fits both of these definitions. He provided an account of the seven churches in Revelation and proved that past prophets' testimonies concerning his birth, life, death, and resurrection were indeed true.

At the beginning of Revelation, our Savior makes an account of the church's actions. These apocalyptical messages were forewarnings from

The Revelation Names of Jesus Christ

Jesus to the churches. As a reliable source, Jesus was able to confirm the churches' exploits and deeds. Despite having righteous acts, Ephesus lost their love for Christ and was warned to repent (Rev 2:1–7), while Smyrna remained faithful during persecution and hardship (Rev 2:8–11). Jesus witnessed the Pergamum church's fall, which returned to worshipping pagan gods (Rev 2:12–17) and Thyatira, who followed false teachings (Rev 2:18–29). On the other hand, Sardis had unfinished deeds because they were alive but spiritually dead (Rev 3:1–6). Jesus also verified the works of Philadelphia, who, despite their limited strength, remained faithful to his words. At the same time, Laodicea seemed to ravish in their wealth versus realizing their disabled state (Rev 3:14–22). Jesus was the only reliable source who could genuinely testify about God's mysteries as he was with him in the beginning and the end.

Being called the Faithful and True Witness indicates the authenticity of the Messianic prophecies that occurred at the beginning of time from Genesis (49:1) to Revelation, confirming that he is the *Amen* or the truth. The word Amen is a Hebrew term that is utilized to convey that something is genuine and authentic. As Christians, we use this word to conclude our prayers to confirm our request before God. Our amen means that the utterance of our heart's desires was sincere and true. As the Amen of God, Jesus displays that God's plan for man's redemption was real and will be fully fulfilled within the last days.

This implementation of God's truth will be accomplished with the reign of our Lord and Savior, Jesus Christ. Past insights revealed that he would be *King of kings and Lord of lords* (Isa 11:10, 1 Tim 6:15 & Rev 15:3). While captive, Jesus told Pontius Pilate that the reason why he was born was that he might be king and "bear witness unto the truth" (John 18:37). This testament distinguished that Jesus was God's Amen, the Faithful Witness, as well as the eternal King. This verse displayed part of the mysteries of God's plan as his Son had to come to earth to die, but later to be crowned king. Earnestly Pilate attempted to save Jesus' life, without knowing that through his death, *his* life would be saved. As King of all kings, he was upholding his ultimate duty to protect the kingdom against his adversary. His death meant that sin could not place any of God's children in a hellish dungeon, but freed them unto eternal life.

Global powers currently exist as we have government officials that rule every part of our world. Presently, these heads of state are working seemingly independently to protect their nations against other foreign threats.

However, there will be times when they will relinquish their powers to one unified system in attempts to overthrow God's Kingdom. Ironically, it is difficult for an influential person to surrender their authority to another, yet in the end, ten will give their power to one. Still, unbeknownst to them, their limited power was already taken at the death of the almighty King. At the sound of the trumpet, Jesus will descend from heaven to claim back his kingdom and will be announced the King of kings and Lord of lords.

This victorious title of Jesus Christ is only one of the names he will have during his reign. Despite previous understandings, God's mysteries are still concealed, evident by the unknown name written on Jesus. Theologians have sought tirelessly to understand the secrecies of this unidentified title. Some believe it references the unique relationship between God and his Son. Whereas others believe it corresponds with previous events in which the angel of the Lord chose not to reveal his name. When Jacob wrestled against the angel, he did not disclose his moniker despite Jacob's inquiry (Gen 32:29). The same occurrence happened when Samson's parents asked for the angel's name that appeared unto them, and the angel replied, "Why do you ask my name? It is beyond understanding" (Judg 13:18 NIV). In other biblical translations, the angel declares that this incomprehensible name is too wondrous also to be mentioned, correlating with Isaiah's prophecy as Jesus's name being *Wonderful* (Isa 9:6).

It appears that within both theories, a single theme arises; the Lord, our God, is too profound for us to understand. The mysteries of God are still yet to be revealed through his Son, Jesus Christ. Within Revelation, we can see the unfolding of these mysterious events, yet it appears that we may never utterly understand the wonder he encompasses. As we review the many names he inherited at the end of days, we know for sure that he was in the beginning as the Word of God to become the slaughtered sacrificial lamb who will regain his kingdom as the ultimate King.

Chapter 9

THE HOLY SPIRIT

And they were all filled with the Holy Ghost, and began to speak with other tongues, as the Spirit gave them utterance.

ACTS 2:4

MOST INDIVIDUALS KNOW LINUS van Pelt, the infamous character in the Peanut cartoon, Charlie Brown. His most prized possession is his blue security blanket. Like a Master Card, he doesn't leave home without it. However, on several occasions, members of the Peanut gang attempt to rob him of his security. Often they failed. However, when successful, Linus' mental health falls into anxiety and depression. Some characters even stated that he doesn't need it, often taunting him to give it up. There were times he tried but failed miserably. For Linus, the security blanket was more than a mere object; but it was a sense of comfort in an unpredictable world.

Imagine how the disciples felt once they learned their "security blanket" would soon be gone. Indeed, they felt like Linus, depressed, panicked, and upset. For three years, the disciples became emotionally attached to Jesus, and now he seemed be leaving them when things were getting harder. Even though Jesus attempted to explain his departure, his explanation fell on deaf ears.

Thomas inquired where he was going, and Philip wanted to know how he could find him. These questions were probably all the disciples' sentiments as Jesus was their leader and guide. Confused, bewildered, and a little frightened, they knew their security would soon be gone. Questionably shaken by Jesus' absence, the disciples experienced separation anxiety even before the separation could occur.

In our lives, we tend to feel like Linus and the disciples when our sense of security is threatened whether it be our family, job, or finances. For Linus, his comfort was in his blanket; however, the disciples' faith was in Jesus. It appears that the disciples had good reason to be a little uneasy with Jesus's pending absence. Without him, life is impossible. However, Jesus promised that even though he was departing, he would leave them with a *Comforter*. It appeared that this Comforter would take Jesus' place as he merely walked with the disciples, but the Holy Spirit would abide in them (John 16:7).

Unfortunately, like Linus, many people have taunted the saints of God to give up the security of the Holy Spirit. They say we don't need it. That the fire that burns with it is a bit too much. Some have even gone to say that it doesn't even exist. Indeed, we could live our lives without the Holy Ghost; however, we would be like Linus, disoriented, depressed, and disillusioned. Like Linus, if we attempt to give the Holy Spirit up, we will fail miserably, living a less abundant life.

Within the Trinity, the Holy Spirit was first defined by Jesus as the Comforter or, in other words, a Helper or Counselor. These terms represent one of the Holy Spirit's principal occupations, guiding us to all truth (John 16:13). When he ascended to heaven, he told the disciples to wait in Jerusalem for the Father's promise (Luke 24:9). Understandably, Jesus knew that the disciples would not be able to stand alone within this world without help. The disciples needed someone to guide and lead them, just as Jesus did while on Earth. Therefore, God would introduce them to another part of the Trinity, which was the Holy Ghost.

Often categorized as a ghost or a spirit, this part of the Godhead is probably one of the most misunderstood out of the three. When we view the Holy Trinity, we understand God, the Father, as he is the Creator of all things. He is El-Shaddai, the Almighty God, the Sovereign One. Within the Godhead, we also understand God the Son, Jesus Christ, the Savior of the World, the soon coming King, the Way, the Truth, and the Light. However, when it comes to the Holy Spirit, we tend to discount his functioning as if he is the lesser part of the Trinity. This is not true, as the Godhead works together equally. When Jesus talked to the disciples, he told them to baptize in the name of the Father, the Son, and the Holy Spirit (Matt 28:19), indicating that the Holy Spirit was not excluded, thus being co-eternal.

The Holy Spirit

There are several misconceptions concerning the Holy Spirit, which causes the church to suffer "Holy Spirit atheism[1]." An atheist does not merely state that there is no god; they simply lack the belief in God. Likewise, many in our churches believe in God the Father and the Son without believing in the Holy Spirit. They recognize that there is a third part of the Trinity, however lack the ability to understand his function. Unfortunately, many Christians state they possess the Holy Spirit, but still do not fully believe in his power. Without understanding the Holy Ghost's capabilities, Christianity has suffered as we lose the God-given authority to change the world.

First, we must recognize despite being called a spirit or a ghost; the Holy Spirit is an actual person with feelings, thoughts, and behaviors. Matthew 28:19 indicates that the Holy Spirit is a part of the Godhead, concluding that he is the third *person* in the Holy Trinity. Most importantly, he is equal to God. Enthusiast against the truth have described him as a detached force from the Father and the Son. Considering that a force is an inanimate object without thoughts or feelings, how can the Holy Spirit be deemed a force when it can grieve, think, and reason (1 Cor 2:10; Rom 15:30; Eph 4:30).

Another misconception is that the Holy Spirit only appeared after Jesus ascended back to the Father. This is debunked as all parts of the Holy Trinity were present at the foundation of the world. Genesis 1:2 states that the earth was dark and without form and the Spirit of God moved upon the waters. Therefore, before the Bible even mentions God the Son, it says the Spirit of God or the Holy Ghost.

Ironically, the Spirit moved over the water and not the void, only because when the Spirit of God moves, it can break and form nothing into something. Naturally, water is the foundation of land formations. And when the Lord's Spirit moved upon the water, the mountains, valleys, canyons, and hills were formed. Therefore, the Spirit produced these formations because of the living water that even moves in our lives today.

Not only this but in Genesis 2:7, God breathed the *Breath of Life* into Adam, who became a living soul. The Hebrew word for breath is spirit, which means that God breathed his spirit into Adam, his life source. God continues to give his breath to the just as well as the unjust. We live today on the breath of the Almighty God as it is not our own, but we borrow it.

---

1. Horan, "The Church," lines 13–16.

Consequently, when the Spirit of God moved upon the water initially, it was able to move to create life in us. Once again, God gave this water to believers as well as unbelievers. Since all humans have the Spirit of Life and water residing in us, we, as Holy Ghost filled believers, have this life more abundantly than those who lack this powerful gift from God.

There is a direct link to water and the Holy Spirit that provides evidence that the Holy Spirit was, in the beginning, moving upon the water. Jesus spoke and said that we should possess rivers of living water flowing out of our bellies if we believe in the Holy Ghost (John 7:37–39). These rivers are not docile, but mighty and stirred up; just like when the angel came down to trouble the pool (John 5:4). The water that comes from the Holy Spirit resides in us, as we no longer have to wait at the bank, as we are the pool.

Another correlation between water and the Holy Spirit also occurs in Isaiah 44:3, which states that God will pour out water on the drylands and our offspring and descendants. If we possess the Holy Spirit, then our familial generations will be blessed as God stated he would pour out. When God pours, he saturates and drenches to the point that the water can flow from generation to generation. The water does not merely flow down, but it also springs up to eternal life (John 4:14). The blessings of the Holy Spirit can reach to our children, but they must receive the Holy Ghost for themselves for the fountain to spring up towards everlasting life. God gave everyone water for survival, but the water that lives inside us was troubled by the Holy Spirit for spiritual living.

Job understood the functions of the Holy Spirit as the agent of life and death. In Job 32:8, he states, "The Spirit of God has made me, and the breath of the Almighty gives me life." In this notion, it appears that Job's attitude resembles the creation of the first man in which God formed from the dust. However, Job understood that the breath of the Holy Spirit gave him life. It is essential to know that just as the Holy Spirit can give life, it can also take it away.

As the Lord directed Noah to collect two of every creature, all that were left died as the breath of life left them. Another incident occurred when Ananias and his wife Sapphira lied to the Holy Spirit, causing them to "give up the ghost" and died before they could even repent (Acts 5:3). The notion of "giving up the ghost" literally means a "dying breath[2]." Conclud-

---

2. "To Give," line 1.

ing that the Holy Spirit has full control over life and has the divine power to give it or take it away.

One of the most well-known illustrations of the Holy Spirit giving life was Ezekiel's prophecy to the dry bones (Ezek 37:1–14). As God told Ezekiel to prophesy to this army of the dead, miraculously, flesh and bones came together, creating lifeless soldiers as no breath was within them. Once again, Ezekiel spoke to the breath, requesting him to breathe on the slain so they may live. Consequently, this was the same breath that blew life into Adam (Gen 2:7). On both occasions, God's life-giving breath created nothing into something, causing that which was once dead to live.

With God's Spirit dwelling in us, it commands us to live in the power of his might (Ezek 37:14). The Spirit of the Almighty God gives us our very existence. Regardless of any dead situations within our lives, the power of the Holy Spirit causes life-awakening phenomena to occur despite the consequences of our limited abilities.

Within the Old Testament, several individuals did extraordinary feats once the Holy Spirit rested on them. The Holy Spirit allowed Othniel to defeat the king of Mesopotamia despite the Israelites being oppressed for eight years (Judg 3:10). Zechariah, who faced death, boldly denied his own life to prophesied judgment to the people (2 Chr 24:20). Gideon was able to defeat the Midianites with only three hundred men after the Spirit of the Lord rested on him (Judg 6:34). Likewise, Samson killed a lion with his bare hands through the Holy Spirit's power (Judg 14:6). Each of these individuals was limited by their own humanly characteristics. However, once the Holy Spirit fell on them, they were able to do outstanding tasks. If these men performed these feats, with the Holy Ghost merely falling on them, then what greater missions can we accomplish if the Holy Ghost abides within us (Rom 8:9–16).

Without the Holy Ghost's divine power, we are powerless and not as productive as we could be for the Kingdom of God. We are in the last days in which Christians state they possess the power of God but seemingly deny its capabilities. It is like a lamp that sits on a table. If the lamp does not turn on, we tend to check the power source, switch out the light bulb, or even change the light switch. Once that lamp does not work, we learn that it is not as effective anymore, and its simple function is décor. That's how it is with Christians who state that they have the power of the Holy Ghost but deny the power thereof (2 Tim 3:5). Proclaiming to have the Holy Spirit dwelling within us means that we never have to check the power source because we know that the power comes from God. Perhaps, we aren't fully connected to the Source and are simply decorating our churches like the ineffectual lamp.

There are two sets of Christians: those who are followers and those who are power-filled followers of Christ. Those who simply follow Christ without the Holy Spirit dwelling in them act on their intuition, thinking that what they do pleases God. They have good intentions but sometimes fall short concerning his will. However, those who possess the Holy Spirit tend to act concerning God's will, despite their own logic.

Peter is a perfect example of a follower of Christ and one who is filled with the Holy Ghost. Before the Day of Pentecost, Peter often acted impulsively, acting on his capabilities and faith. When he saw Jesus walking on water, he was the first to get out of the boat to attempt to walk on the sea. Some believe this act was a faith walk, but it showed Peter's impulsiveness. He could have easily waited for instructions like the other eleven; instead, he walked out and began to sink (Matt 14:22–33). On another occasion, Jesus asked the disciples who men believed he was, and the disciples gave answers. However, Peter proclaimed Jesus to be the Son of the Living God. Jesus was pleased with Peter's response and said he would be the rock that the church would be built. However, within the same conversation, Jesus called Peter Satan, stating, "you are an offense unto me" because Peter was discounting what Jesus was saying about his upcoming suffering and the will of God (Mark 16:15–23).

However, once Peter was filled with the Holy Ghost, he acted impulsively for God's will and not his own. Peter was able to boldly proclaim the Holy Spirit's truth and the events that would follow for those who believed. As the people listened to Peter, he converted three thousand people to salvation with the confluence of the Holy Ghost. Peter was now a power-filled follower of Christ, acting on the Lord's behalf and getting more outstanding results than following his own will (Acts 2).

The Holy Spirit brings forth divine power to accomplish the will of God (Acts 1:8). Power is "the capacity or ability to direct or influence others' behavior or the course of events." These works occurred with Jesus as he was full of the Spirit, but they also can occur within us. The Holy Spirit abides in our bodies, and we can do far more than we could ever accomplish on our own. The miracles that Jesus performed were not only limited to him as the Son of God, but we have that same power dwelling in us today. Just as Jesus healed the sick, so can we. If Jesus was able to raise the dead, then we have this same power. Our ability is only limited by our physical incapability that says we cannot. However, if we as Christians believe that we can be resurrected, then we must also believe in the divine powerful abilities that live in us today.

Within the Old Testament, many patriarchs were successful without having the Holy Spirit living within them. However, since we now have the Holy Ghost abiding within, then greater works can we accomplish. David was a great leader in the old testament who won many battles with only the Holy Spirit resting on him. Even with his extraordinary accomplishments, he was limited because the Holy Ghost was not dwelling in him. However, to his credit, Paul was filled with the Holy Ghost and converted many Jews and Gentiles to Christ. This same spirit that allowed David to obtain his victories by merely following him is the same spirit that lives inside us, ready to proclaim our triumphs. Being filled with the Spirit ignites miracles, signs, and wonders, yet we use it with limitations.

Perhaps we cannot activate the full power of the Spirit because we lack knowledge of the Holy Ghost. The Holy Spirit is a gift with many functions and capabilities. Several Christians have received this gift from God. Unfortunately, they have not unraveled its mysteries. We allow the Spirit of God to rest inside of us dormant because we're not willing to ignite the power. This is like leaving a valuable present unwrapped under the Christmas tree. The gift has already been purchased, just waiting to be opened. So, it is with the Holy Spirit. The Holy Spirit lives inside of us, ready to have full operation, yet we merely claim to have it, versus operating truly in it. God has freely given us the Spirit to fully understand the many gifts under the umbrella of the Holy Ghost (1 Cor 2:12).

Understanding the Holy Spirit's nine contributions will help us examine how this part of the Godhead works in our lives. Knowledge, wisdom, prophecy, faith, healings, working miracles, discerning spirits, tongues, and their interpretation are all gifts from the Holy Ghost. It is the belief that every Christian who claims to have the inhabitation of the Spirit has at least one of these gifts or, at the very least able to operate in them periodically. According to First Corinthians 12:7–11, the Holy Spirit distributes these gifts to each power-filled believer as he sees fit. Furnishing these endowments of the spirit is for all individuals' uplifting and should be utilized to profit us all (Rom 12:6).

Knowledge and wisdom are two corresponding gifts of the Spirit that seeks to provide understanding. Daily the Holy Spirit gives us knowledge about trivial issues to essential awareness of God's Word. Knowledge is one of the gifts that work within us consistently as the Holy Spirit brings things to our remembrance (John 14:26). Often Christians think of this verse relating to misplaced items, however what about when our goodness is absent. The Holy Spirit is more than a car key finder, but it will help believers regain appropriate behaviors and thoughts. It guides us to maintain a rightful relationship with God.

Wisdom, on the contrary, helps us apply that knowledge to a higher level of thinking. For example, our knowledge of money tells us that we need it to purchase and buy items; however, wisdom will tell us how to spend it. Our knowledge of God's Word is foundational, and wisdom increases the growth of the application. Without these two gifts working together, we would lack comprehension of necessary life-sustaining information and understandings on spiritual operations.

Acting in full knowledge of God will increase the Holy Spirit's next gift, which is faith. Each Christian has been given a measure of faith as by which we are saved (Eph 2:8–9). Faith first comes by God; then, the Holy Spirit begins to manifest this gift within our lives. Faith is the substance of things hoped and the evidence of things not seen (Heb 11:1). As we learn how to walk in the Spirit, we also learn how-to walk-in faith. Believing in God is not a one-time occurrence for salvation, yet it is a stepping stone to a more remarkable journey. It is an everlasting gift of continued praise, worship, and love despite not seeing God (1 Pet 1:8–9). Walking by faith and not by sight allows us the knowledge and wisdom to fully put our confidence in an unseen Being (2 Cor 5:7). Our faith gift will enable us to see spiritual awareness without being limited by our physical sight.

Spiritual awareness is another gift of the spirit, which is called prophecy. Some Christians have temporary acts of this gift, while some entirely operate in it. Prophecy is not merely foretelling future events, but it also provides correcting, comfort, divine revelations, and bold proclamations of God's Word. Paul admonished all believers to seek spiritual gifts, but especially after prophecy (1 Cor 14:1). Those who function in this gift hear directly from God. Their job is to be the "mouthpiece" for him, disclosing the church's truth and enlightment (1 Cor 14:3–4, 24–25). This divine gift connects the church to God, allowing him to communicate with his people continuously.

Others in the church may have the gift of discerning of Spirits. This gift allows individuals to distinguish between spirits that are and are not of

God. Operating in discernment helps protect the church from false prophets and demonic forces that attempt to override God's will. Our adversary is cunning and devious, working his way into the hearts of not just unbelievers but believers as well to 'steal, kill, and destroy" the divine plans of God. Individuals with this gift can sense the demonic beings more than any other Christian as they tend not to make bold appearances. They camouflage themselves waiting for the perfect time to stir discord individually, within a person, or collectively, disrupting the church body. Individuals with this unique gift can see past the disguise and reveal the presented evil.

Even though discernment detects wickedness, it can also see the spirits that are for God. Often people operating in this gift can sense a shifting in the atmosphere that allows God to move in mighty ways among his people. These believers are in tune with the Holy Spirit and should communicate to the congregation the spirit's flow. Sharing that angels are among us or that Shekinah glory has rested in the tabernacle allows everyone to get on one accord within the Spirit of God.

When we are on one accord, then miracles and healings can occur within the church. Both are gifts from the Holy Spirit, which can manifest themselves in believers. Miracles happened within the Bible on several occasions, such as the ten plagues of Egypt (Exod 7:20–12:30), the mass murder of the Assyrian army (2 Kgs 19:35), and the feeding of five thousand people (Matt 14:15). Just as healing was demonstrated both in the old and new testament as many regained sight, were cured of diseases, and raised from the dead, he continues to heal today. God works these miracles to demonstrate his omnipotent power that we may further believe in his superior capabilities. Every believer has the privilege of having these gifts as God sees fit. Often, he will give these gifts as needed while others possess the gift of healing continuously.

Notice in First Corinthians 12:9 it states the gifts of healing, in which the word gift is plural. Signifying that believers can work with different types of healings and diseases. One believer could have the advantage of healing arthritis, while another psychological issues, and another cancer. God allows each believer to operate in this gift according to one's faith. As the children of God, we should seek after the gift of healing as God wants to heal his people of physical and mental ailments that were caused by the Adamic covenant.

Another gift that believers should request is the gift of tongues and their interpretation. When the gift of tongues is activated, it can show forth in two different forms. The first one allows a believer to communicate in a foreign language that they did not study to help people believe in God, such as the Day of Pentecost. The other manifestation is when one speaks a heavenly language specifically to God. This communication allows us to directly link with the Father as the Holy Spirit becomes our prayer guide. This conversation is so exclusive that we don't even know what we are saying. "For he who speaks in a tongue does not speak to men but God, for no one, understands him; however, in the spirit, he speaks mysteries" (1 Cor 14:2). What a powerful gift to possess as we have a spokesperson that speaks on our behalf. Especially when we don't know how to pray; he will intercede for us (Rom 8:26). Even though we have this communicational gift, we should also understand what our spirit is saying to God. Paul admonished that all believers who have the gift of tongues also pray for interpretation as both skills are twofold. It is good to have one, but it is best to have both to access our prayers' real power completely.

Before we can activate our gifts, we must possess the characteristics of God, which the Holy Ghost will produce within us. Despite God making us all in his image, many people will not contain the same godly characteristics or the spirit's divine fruits. In the natural, all fruit is labeled as such but does not taste the same. So, it is with God's creation. The Spirit of God helps us further mature in these fruits as we become more in the image of our Father. This growth takes time and does not occur overnight. No one wants to eat an unripe fruit as it is harder to digest, which causes digestive problems and can be toxic. When Christians do not have God's characteristics, it is harder for them to digest the Word often causing them to regurgitate, leading to deadly consequences. Thankfully, we have a divine gardener in God whose careful guidance helps produce the best possible fruit within us. Often weeds will come up that God has to pluck out, and pruning must occur for further growth. Nevertheless, through the Holy Spirit, the fruit grows, generating Christians in the most fabulous image of God.

Love is one of the essential traits given by our heavenly Father. Our entire foundation of salvation is based upon it. Since God is love, love has been at the very launch of our existence. God's love did not destroy Adam and Eve after they rejected the truth, and that same agape love continues to show mercy towards all creation. It binds us all in perfect harmony (Col 3:14) as Paul even admonishes us to do all things with love (1 Cor 16:14). The Spirit of God produces love within us that is unlike the love of this world. Being that it resides with us, it delivers patience and kindness, seeking out the truth, never failing (1 Cor 13:4-8). Therefore, God has placed this love inside of our hearts that will never cease to end.

With this love comes other invaluable traits such as joy and peace. Joy only happens for those in the world when nothing is going wrong. This trait is solely based upon their circumstances. However, Paul said that we should have joy even during hardship as it is only testing our faith, making us stronger (Jas1:1-2). Oddly, this seems unfathomable to be happy when our finances are depleting, our marriages are on the verge of ending, and life utterly seems hopeless.

Nevertheless, God produces peace in our lives, commanding the storm winds to cease. The peace of God surpasses all understanding; it's genuinely unconceivable (Phil4:7). Regardless of the situation, God's peace entangles us to the point that we find ourselves smiling even while facing horrendous potential outcomes. As Christians, we simply stand on our Father's words that we can cast our cares on him because he cares for us (1 Pet 5:7).

Challenges will arise within our lives, but thankfully God has given us the fruit of forbearance. This word is often translated as patience, longsuffering, or perseverance. Experiencing adversity in life would cause anyone to feel like throwing in the towel. However, through the Holy Spirit, we can stand any wicked spiritual powers that arise (Eph 6:10-17). We have an everlasting endurance as our Heavenly Father is longsuffering and slow to anger (Ps 103:8). Imaginably, we do not think of God as suffering as he is God. However, he suffers with our sins, and he delays his wrath from us despite our justification of it (Isa 48:9). Having the Holy Spirit allows us to follow in our Father's footsteps showing forth kindness and mercy, just as God demonstrates to us all (Col 3:13).

Jesus spoke of a parable of an unmerciful servant who was forgiven of a large debt from his master. However, this servant could not forgive someone who owed him substantially less (Matt 18:21-35). Unfortunately, the same fate that he gave to his servant was given to him because he lacked the spirit of kindness. Ephesians 4:32 states, "Be kind to one another, tenderhearted, forgiving each other, just as God in Christ also has forgiven you." Kindness goes beyond being pleasant to one another, but it also decreases our judgmental mentalities. Understanding and showing empathy versus being self-righteous is the foundation of this fruit of the spirit.

By being kind, we allow the *Spirit of Meekness* to encompass our lives. Our Savior was a perfect example of this characteristic. Under the direst circumstance, Jesus was humiliated and mistreated, yet he humbly died on the cross with little concern for himself but showed forth concern for others. This character trait is often seen as a sign of feebleness; however, "meekness is not weakness." Jesus had the power and could have called legions of angels to rescue him. However, his meekness was "power under control."

Demonstrating gentleness can allow others to reconsider their transgressions and lead them to a closer relationship with Christ. At Calvary, Jesus' answers and behaviors during his dreadful death caused the thief on the cross to consider his sins and was converted because of meekness. Our actions and communication can lead others to Christ without demonstrating aggressiveness. Think of what would have happened if Jesus showed forth his divine power while on the cross. He could have easily destroyed all his accusers and still died, but that one soul would probably have been lost.

Several Christians underestimate this character trait because it does not seem to demonstrate power. However, meekness has a quiet strength that only Christians can possess. Think about Moses, whose anger caused him to kill a man. This act of hatred did not profit the kingdom anything. However, once the Spirit of God introduced himself to Moses, Moses was considered the meekest man in all the world (Num12:3). Moses allowed the Spirit to follow and direct him even during judgment and persecution. Converting a murderer to a meek man is nothing short of what the Holy Spirit can do for the people of God. By obtaining meekness, Moses could accomplish more for God than he could ever do by exhibiting aggression and hostility.

Our behaviors and communication can lead others to Christ without demonstrating anger. God's system is different from the world's as real power remains quiet during mistreatment and oppression. Moses' critics were his brother and sister, yet instead of making way for sibling rivalry, Moses remained quiet, trusting God. It takes a stronger individual to possess meekness than one that seeks out his own vengeance. The Spirit of God gives us self-control, which restricts our thoughts and behaviors, bringing forth a greater strength. Romans 12:14 tells us to bless those who persecute instead of seeking out revenge. A meek man will trust in God to defend them versus them defending themselves. God said that vengeance is his, and he would repay (Rom 12:19). Our retaliation is nothing compared to what God has in store for those who harm his children.

Systematic beliefs of the world are based upon power and assertiveness that people use to gain worldly wealth and prestige. Since we are not of this world, Christians possess Godly confidence as we believe in the Lord. Psalms 37:9–11 states that those who hope and put their trust in God will inherit the earth, which was confirmed by Jesus during the Sermon on the Mount, in which he authorized the meek's earthly inheritance (Matt 5:5). The parallels between these Scriptures suggest that the meek wait and place their trust in the Most High. Our spiritual inheritance is centered around this characteristic as we will not be able to gain eternal life without first trusting and then waiting on God. As Christians, we should place our confidence in God over our finances or our abilities. Any control or power that we possess does not come from degrees, employment, or election, but through God. Our reliance is that we can rest assured that our spiritual possessions and status are covered through our meekness.

By possessing this quality, not only shall we inherit the earth, but the meek will also gain peace (Ps 37:11) and salvation (Ps 149:4). Jesus counted himself as meek and lowly in heart, giving us a clear example of this attribute (Matt 11:29). Before he was born, it was prophesied that "the chastisement of our peace was upon him" (Isa 53:5). Since we were born in sin, our nature creates turmoil and anarchy, including the war against ourselves. Each day, our physical bodies battle with our spirit as our flesh is full of sin. It appears that the law of good and evil happens each day as we want to do good, but evil is always present (Rom 7:21). Our sinful nature just doesn't battle against others and ourselves, but we war against the Holy Word. It is our human character to challenge God, and without the Holy Spirit producing this fruit, we would not have a full relationship with him.

Reconciliation was needed between man and God for us to acquire peace. Without Jesus humbling himself to the cross, the world would suffer great pandemonium far worse than it is today. Imagine the mayhem and chaos our society would have endured if it had not been for the meekness of Jesus, who made no reputation for himself but became his creation to die for our sins (Phil2:5). Adorning ourselves in this incorruptible ornament will allow the Holy Spirit to humble our hearts and accept peace into our lives. Paul admonished that all believers seek peace with all men (Rom 12:18). Seeking peace demonstrates the meekness that our Lord and Savior exhibited during his death. Without this act of meekness, our salvation would have been lost, and tranquility would have been nonexistent.

Granted, when we become saved, our world will not be centered around peace. There is ongoing warfare that attempts to disrupt our calm. Henceforth, discord does not stop once salvation enters our lives;

sometimes, it appears our situation even gets worst. However, our spiritual goal is to continually grow in the knowledge of God to increase our peace. Possessing the Holy Spirit will allow this fruit to manifest itself in our lives as it goes beyond the world's definition.

Peace for unbelievers is a sense of stillness and tranquility when everything is going right. However, peace for the Children of God is despite the hardship that we face; we still have established a peace of mind because of the confidence that we have in him. He tells us in our world that he has given us God-given peace that transcends all understanding. Our hearts should never be troubled as the *Spirit of Peace* dwells within our soul (John 14:27).

Peace is one of the fruits of the Spirit God-ordained within his Son by calling him the "Prince of Peace." Our peace with God only comes through and by our Lord and Savior, Jesus Christ (Rom 5:1). Our warfare against sin could not be fought in physical combat as we are too weak and feebleminded. Therefore, he sent his Son to bring peace to the world that he could end the war of sin. Jesus coming to earth was the first part of the battle plan as he taught believers how-to live-in peace. Even under the direst situations, Jesus humbled himself and sought peace with all he encountered. The second part of his plan was for his Son to die. The goal was to ensure everlasting peace between God and believers. Despite our sinful nature, the death of Jesus Christ cleansed us from iniquity, allowing for a restored relationship with the Father.

Gratefully this reconciliation has also allowed us to witness and partake of the sevenfold ministry in the Holy Ghost. As Isaiah prophesied about the coming Messiah, he verbalized that he would possess the Lord's Spirit along with the Spirit of wisdom and understanding, the Spirit of counsel and might, the Spirit of knowledge, and the fear of the Lord (Isa 11:2). Ironically, Jesus was indeed full of the Spirit, meaning that Jesus operated in these seven. Undeniably, there is only one Spirit, yet we find in Revelation that under the umbrella of the Holy Spirit are these seven (Rev 1:4, 3:1, 4:5, 5:6). Just like the Father, Son, and Holy Ghost are separate deities forming the Godhead, the Holy Spirit, and the seven are one. It is believed that we must also function within these listed spirits for us to be used entirely by the Holy Ghost.

This does not mean that the Holy Spirit does not work in us. However, it does appear that many possess limited power. The Holy Spirit is a power source that dwells in believers' bodies, yet we are not witnessing full manifestations of this authority because we lack as the people of God. We may operate with the knowledge of God but lack the wisdom in how to apply that knowledge. Likewise, we may possess the Holy Spirit, but reluctantly or unwillingly allow it to use us in peculiar ways, thus lacking fear of the Lord. As Isaiah's prophecy came to pass, we can quickly see how Jesus was able to perform miracles as he entirely operated within the seven spirits mentioned.

Having the *Lord's Spirit* is a unique understanding that a person must experience and know for themselves. As Jesus was preparing to go to a village in Samaria, the Samaritans did not necessarily place a welcome mat at the city gates for our Messiah. Instead, they rejected him, which offended his disciples. James and John wanted to take immediate action and use God's power like Elijah did, causing fire to rain down on these ungrateful people. However, Jesus rebuked them, saying, "You do not know what manner of spirit you are of" (John 9:51–55). James and John desired to use the power of God with the wrong motives. However, since he had the Lord's Spirit, he explained his Father's will to save lives versus destroying them. When the Spirit of the Lord resides in a person, there is a complete understanding and acknowledgment that there is a power that is teaching, guiding, and directing them in full operation of God.

Jesus not only demonstrated that he had the Lord's spirit, but he also showed the *Spirit of Wisdom*. It would have been absurdity if Jesus said he was sent here as a Savior but used his power to extinguish those who rejected him. If this were the case, then billions would have been abolished from the earth. Nevertheless, Jesus understood that wisdom allows God to direct us even during difficult and even emotional situations. As Christians, we are human and subjected to act with our emotions instead of consulting God. The reason why we do this is because we want instantaneous vengeance; we want microwave results. However, God takes his time to revenge us. This does not mean that God acts slowly; we just recognize that his timetable is different than ours. Therefore, if we utilize godly wisdom, then we can have better results. A microwavable impact does not taste better than a slow-cooked oven planned solution. As God's people, we must seek the Spirit of Wisdom as Jesus did not only have wisdom, but he is the definition of it (1 Cor 1:30).

Having godly wisdom also correlates to having divine understanding. The *Spirit of Understanding* allows Christians to meet unbelievers where they are in their sin. When we were first saved, we did not resemble God.

We looked exactly, if not worse, than the sinner we are attempting to bring to Christ. Jesus could have easily caused fire and brimstone to rain on the Samaritan village; however, he understood their reasonings. Jesus was a Jew, and within Samaritan culture, Jews were not necessarily welcomed. This feud had taken place during the civil unrest during the division of the Southern and Northern Kingdoms (1 Kgs 12:16–24; 15:6). Since the Samaritans began to worship idol gods and participated in intermarriages, the Jews despised how they turned away from God (Deut 7:3–5). Despite this, Jesus still recognized but most importantly validated the Samaritan's villages' reasons for not welcoming necessarily the Messiah, but a Jew. Having the Spirit of Understanding will help us realize that people may not be ready to receive the gospel when it is presented. Instead of forcing judgment, enforce understanding as this is an essential part of winning souls to Christ.

Jesus came to this world that he may give us abundant life through his saving grace. However, another reason is that Jesus wanted to prove that we can live a life free from sin. Our Savior understands our weaknesses and our temptations, as he also went through the same things we dwell with today. It's tough to imagine Jesus being tempted with illegal substances or sexual immorality; however, it happened. Hebrews 4:15 states that he was tempted at all points, yet he never sinned. Our hindrances or stumbling blocks that keep us from fulfilling the will of God is understandable but not excusable. Jesus had to suffer every temptation known to man for him to have a greater understanding of the obstacles we encounter. Therefore, he is our great intercessor, always fighting on our behalf. The Lord understands where we are but expects that we grow in grace and full knowledge of him (2 Pet 3:18).

Even as the Son of God, Jesus had to have knowledge; in fact, he is the epitome of it. Jesus Christ is the Word, and hearing or reading the Word brings knowledge, thus concluding that Jesus Christ is full of this spirit. Possessing the *Spirit of Knowledge* connects us to a greater understanding of who God is, but equivalently who we are in him. If we understand the Father's power and authority, then we can understand the power and authority granted to us. As Christians, we are limited within the Holy Ghost's power because we lack knowledge of what is genuinely abiding within us.

God has given us the light of knowledge to understand his great power (2 Cor 4:6-7). However, we are weak in our understanding or do not fully believe the power and authority that has been granted by the Holy Ghost.

Once we receive the divine knowledge, we can walk within our spiritual authority to heal the sick, cast out demonic spirits, and raise the dead (Matt 10:1). Ironically, some of us comprehend that we have this authority; however, this powerful application is negligent.

Inquiring the *Spirit of Might*, allows Christians to operate in our knowledge of the Holy Spirit and apply this power. Unfortunately, this spirit often sits docile within the body of Christ as it is the utilization of the power of the Holy Ghost. It is our strength and influence within the church and outside of it. Our God is a mighty warrior, strong in battle, and never once did he ever lose a fight.

We have this knowledge that our God is who we say he is, yet what about his children. If our God is mighty, full of bravery and capabilities, why do we resemble a scared child, hiding behind his shirttail? The Lord has given us the power to trample over spiritual serpents and scorpions that try to poison us against what God said concerning our victories. We do not merely walk on them, but we crush their ideologies of doubt and fear through the power of God's might (Luke 10:19). We never have to be afraid of our enemies as God has already prepared our victory feast. He just waits for us to show up at the table (Ps 23:5).

The only thing we must do is pronounce these blessings in our lives. We have the power to overcome the battle of poverty, rejection, mental illness, disease, and demonic spirits as our weapon is the Holy Ghost. These spirits must stand in subjection to the Holy Spirit that is abiding within us. Our God is mighty; therefore, we as his children have this might dwelling on the inside. We must exercise the power of the Holy Spirit to go into battle against what the enemy says or believes about our situations. The only voice that matters is the voice of the Almighty God who proclaims victory. If God is for us, then who can genuinely attempt to stop the battle plan of God? It is time to rise within the power of his might and believe what God says is ours is ours.

No true warrior goes into battle without a plan of attack. Therefore, the *Spirit of Counsel* is the guide that directs us in pursuing our victories. The power of counsel and might correlate with one another as we can possess the ability; however, if we do not know how to use it appropriately, it is useless. Every soldier has a captain that guides them as they enter the battle. Before they go into war, they wait on their general's direction, putting their confidence in them to lead to victory.

God is our mighty captain who is the *Spirit of Truth*, that will guide us in all matters (John 16:13). As his faithful army, we must listen to his counsel to escape the trap of the enemy. Even when we think we are defeated and ensnared, the Holy Spirit will teach and direct us in that very hour on what we should say and do (Luke 12:11-12). All we must do is listen to the advisement of the Holy Spirit that will lead us to our manifested victories.

Victory does not come by fearing our enemies but fearing God. As Christians, we can look at this verb in two manners; either we can be afraid of God or be in awe of him. Each of these definitions can apply to the Lord, however, not our adversary. God did not grant us a spirit of fear, but he gave us power, love, and self-control (2 Tim 1:7). Since the Holy Spirit has given us power, then being afraid of our enemy is pointless. Our fear is simply misplaced because it is not directed towards God.

It is incredible how we fear failure, rejection, change, and even success; when God commands us not to be afraid because we are called by his name (Isa 43:1). God is greater than our failures, rejection, and successes, yet we do not recognize his divine power. Some even fear losing their money versus losing their eternal soul. Thankfully, we understand that fearing God allows us to conquer our natural fears due to his unlimited power within the earth.

Remarkably, God has placed some of this power within us. By having the Holy Spirit, we no longer are simply followers of Christ, but we become power-filled disciples. We relinquish our partial control for unrestrained power through and by the Holy Ghost. There is no greater power in all the earth that humans can possess than having the Spirit of God dwelling on the inside. Maintaining this power means that we have direct communication with God, and most importantly, God has direct contact with us. Revelations and wisdom come from the Holy Spirit, which helps believers understand the manifested power that reigns inside of them. With the Holy Spirit guiding, teaching, and leading the children of God, we can change this entire world. However, we must be obedient to the Spirit of God, stand back, and then watch God perform on our behalf.

Epilogue

OUR VOCABULARIES ARE TOO limited to describe a God that is beyond description. We can call God almighty, gracious, powerful, splendid, but even these words seem to fall short when explaining the magnificence of God and his Son. Perhaps the reasoning is because God is understandable and unconceivable at the same time. As Christians, we should seek to know more about him, but instantaneously we could study for a lifetime and never fully comprehend his glory, power, and might.

The knowledge of him surpasses the scope of our imaginations as our devotion seems ill-equipped when we try to define his splendor. It seems we will never understand him because there are so many layers, thus the many names given to God. However, that does not mean that we should stop trying. There is an unknown name that astonishingly may summarize the characteristics of Jesus, yet it may never be revealed. Our best attempt at genuinely getting to know God is to ensure that we reign with him when he returns.

Bibliography

"Abba." New World Encyclopedia. https://www.newworldencyclopedia.org/entry/Abba.

"Are there rocks in chewing gum?" Ledfrog. https://www.ledfrog.com/miscellaneous/2009/12/are-there-rocks-in-chewing-gum/.

American Bible Society. 1976. Good news Bible: The Bible in Today's English version. New York: American Bible Society.

"Begotten." Vocabulary. https://www.vocabulary.com/dictionary/begotten.

"Covenant - Beriyth (Hebrew Word Study)," Precept Austin. https://www.preceptaustin.org/covenant_definition.

"Daily Bible Study - The Names of God." Divine Bible Names. https://divinebiblenames.blogspot.com/2013/01/study-number-37-jehovah-elohay-lord-my.html.

"Discovery of gigantic 'planet' baffles astronomers." RT News. https://www.rt.com/news/409328-massive-planet-ogle-2016-blg-1190lb/.

Ehrman, Bart. 2014. "Why Romans Crucified People (The Story Beyond the Cross & Nails)." https://ehrmanblog.org/why-romans-crucified-people/.

"'El Emunah," Bibliatodo. https://www.bibliatodo.com/en/names-of-God/el-emunah.

"Elah Sh'maya V'Arah," Bibliatodo. https://www.bibliatodo.com/en/names-of-God/elah-shmaya-varah.

"El Bethel," The Abarim Publications. https://www.abarim-publications.com/Meaning/El-bethel.html.

"El' Elohe Yisrael," The Abarim Publications. https://www.abarim-publications.com/Meaning/El-Elohe-Israel.html.

"El Nathan," The Abarim Publications. https://www.abarim-publications.com/Meaning/Elnathan.html

"El Shama: A God who hears, He is a God who listens," The End Times. https://the-end-time.org/2017/03/25/el-shama-a-god-who-hears-he-is-a-god-who-listens/#:~:text=Though%20%E2%80%98El%20Shama%E2%80%99%20is%20not%20an%20official%20name,el%20and%20shama%2C%20%E2%80%9CGod%20hears%E2%80%9D%20or%20%E2%80%9CGod%20listens%E2%80%9D.

"Elohay Elohim," God's Names. Meaning of ELOHAY ELOHIM - God's names (bibliatodo.com).

"Elohim Chaiyim," God's Names. https://www.bibliatodo.com/en/names-of-God/elohay-chaiyim.

"Elohay Selichot," God's Names. https://www.bibliatodo.com/en/names-of-God/elohay-selichot.

"'El Rachum," Bibliatodo. https://www.bibliatodo.com/en/names-of-God/el-rachum

Bibliography

English Standard Version Bible. 2001. ESV Online. https://esv.literalword.com/.

Evans, Tony. "Praying (and Pronouncing) the Names of God," https://tonyevans.org/praying-and-pronouncing-the-names-of-god/.

"Fourty-four El Names of God." Prayer Today. http://www.prayertoday.org/2013/PDF/2014-44%20El-%20Names%20&%2044%20Jehovah%20Names.pdf.

Francis, Pat. "Chayi Glory in Solomon," https://www.patfrancis.org/dr-pat-francis/chayil-glory-in-solomon-5/#:~:text=One%20of%20the%20descriptive%20names%20of%20God%20is,prayer%2C%20obedience%29%20and%20men%20%28influence%29.%E2%80%9D%20%28Luke%202%3A52%2C%20amplified%29.

Furtick, Steven. "The Pastor's Workshop." https://thepastorsworkshop.com/sermon-quotes-by-topic/sermon-quotes-obedience/.

Gandhi, Mahatma. "Brainy Quotes." https://www.brainyquote.com/quotes/mahatma_gandhi_121411

Gills, N.S. 2020. "List of Gods and Goddesses From Antiquity." https://www.learnreligions.com/list-of-gods-and-goddesses-by-culture-118503

"God of Deliverances," Names for God. https://namesforgod.net/god-of-deliverances/.

"Hebrew Names of God: Adonai and Adonai Construct given in the Tanakh." Hebrew 4 Christians. https://hebrew4christians.com/Names_of_G-d/Adonai/adonai.html#:~:text=Introduction%20Adonai%20is%20the%20plural%20of%20Adon%2C%20meaning,the%20LORD%20God%20of%20Israel%20%28e.g.%2C%20Exodus%2034%3A23%29.

"Hebrew Names of God in The Bible." Biblical Hebrew. https://biblicalhebrew.org/hebrew-names-of-god-in-the-bible.aspx.

Horan, Daniel. "The church is suffering from Holy Spirit atheism." https://www.ncronline.org/news/opinion/faith-seeking-understanding/church-suffering-holy-spirit-atheism.

"Jacob." Behind The Name, 2020. Meaning, origin and history of the name Jacob - Behind the Name.

Jain, Sudeep. 2016. "Preventing chronic neck pain," http://sudeepjain1.blogspot.com/2016/03/preventing-chronic-neck-pain.html.

"Jehovah's Names," Prayer Today. http://www.prayertoday.org/NamesofGod/Jehovah-names.htm.

"John." Mama Natural, 2020. https://www.mamanatural.com/baby-names/boys/john/.

"Joshua." Behind the Name. https://www.behindthename.com/name/joshua#:~:text=From%20the%20Hebrew%20name%20%D7%99%D6%B0%D7%94%D7%95%D6%B9%D7%A9%D6%BB%D7%81%D7%A2%D6%B7,was%20a%20companion%20of%20Moses.&text=As%20an%20English%20name%2C%20Joshua,use%20since%20the%20Protestant%20Reformation.

"Illegitimate." Merriam-Webseter Dictionary. https://www.merriam-webster.com/dictionary/illegitimate

"Is NASA's budget less than 2 percent of the federal budget?" Ballotpedia. https://ballotpedia.org/Fact_check/Is_NASA%27s_budget_less_than_2_percent_of_the_federal_budget.

Kagan, Julia. 2020. "Pay Yourself First." https://www.investopedia.com/terms/p/payyourselffirst.asp.

Khokhar, Sana. "Names for God in the Bible." Names for God in the Bible- All about Bible.

King James Bible. 2020. King James Bible Online. https://www.kingjamesbibleonline.org.

Bibliography

Lamm, Maurice. "The Jewish Marriage Contract (Ketubah)." https://www.chabad.org/library/article_cdo/aid/465168/jewish/The-Jewish-Marriage-Contract-Ketubah.htm.

Leake, Mark. "What does Elohim mean and Why is this name of God so important?". https://www.biblestudytools.com/bible-study/topical-studies/elohim-supreme-one-mighty-one.html.

"Logos." Britannica. https://www.britannica.com/topic/logos.

"Lucifer." Britannica. https://www.britannica.com/topic/Lucifer-classical-mythology.

Lugin, Robert. "Explanation of the Ichthys Symbol and Acronym." https://ichthys.com/ichthys-explanation.htm.

Mark, Joshua. 2017. Ancient Egyptian Symbols. https://www.worldhistory.org/article/1011/ancient-egyptian-symbols/.

Merritt, Daniel. 2019. "What does only begotten son mean?" https://drdanmerritt.com/2019/10/04/what-does-only-begotten-son-mean/.

Meyers, Joyce. "Putting God First in Your Priorities." https://joycemeyer.org/everydayanswers/ea-teachings/putting-god-first-in-your-priorities.

Meyers, Mckenna. 2000. "Fatherless Daughters: How Growing Up Without a Father Impacts Women's Wellbeing." https://wehavekids.com/family-relationships/When-Daddy-Dont-Love-Their-Daughters-What-Happens-to-Women-Whose-Fathers-Werent-There-for-Them

Microsoft Bing Dictionary. "Be." https://www.bing.com/search?q=intransitive%20verb%20of%20be%20means%20%22to%20exist.%22%20%20&qs=n&form=QBRE&sp=-1&pq=intransitive%20verb%20of%20be%20means%20%22to%20exist.%22%20&sc=0-42&sk=&cvid=3ADFE48DA2974ACB9BB25175C5119315.

Miller, Arthur. 1953. The crucible, a play in four acts. New York: Viking.

"Names of God." All about God. https://www.allaboutgod.com/names-of-god.htm

"Names of God." Names of God. https://www.namesofgod.ch/en/54/god-of-life.

"Names of God: 'El Shaddai." I love Jesus. https://iloveijesus.wordpress.com/2014/04/21/names-of-god-el-shaddai/.

New International Version Bible. (2011). The NIV Bible. https://www.thenivbible.com (Original work published 1978).

"Nicene Creed: The Holy Spirit, Neglected but not Forgotten," Highland Park Presbyterian Church." https://www.hppres.org/stories-blogs/posts/nicene-creed-the-holy-spirit.

"Omni." Your Dictionary. https://www.yourdictionary.com/omni.

Opfer, Chris. "What if Earth changed its orbit?" https://science.howstuffworks.com/science-vs-myth/what-if/what-if-earth-changed-its-orbit.htm#:~:text=Even%20a%20small%20move%20closer,Earth%20would%20continue%20to%20rise.

"Our." Your Dictionary. https://www.yourdictionary.com/our.

Parke, Blair. "Yeshua: Deliverer, Savior - Why This Name of God Is So Important for Today." https://www.biblestudytools.com/bible-study/topical-studies/yeshua-deliverer-savior.html.

Parson, John. 2020. "The Name 'El Shaddai." The Name El Shaddai... – Hebrew for Christians (hebrew4christians.com).

"Peter." Behind the Name, 2020. https://www.behindthename.com/name/peter.

"Rabbi." Britannica. https://www.britannica.com/topic/rabbi.

Ratnam, Gauri. 60 Saint Names for Baby Girls. https://parenting.firstcry.com/articles/60-saint-names-for-baby-girls/.

Bibliography

"Saving and Redeeming: An Overview of the Contrast." Turning to God's Word. https://turningtogodsword.com/redemption/

"Renee." Think Baby Names, 2021. http://www.thinkbabynames.com/meaning/0/Renee.

"Repentance, A Word Study." Word. https://cmmorrison.wordpress.com/tag/metanoeo/.

Richman, Chaim. 2013. The King is in the field. https://www.jpost.com/Opinion/Op-Ed-Contributors/The-king-is-in-the-field-322367#:~:text=A%20popular%20rabbinic%20teaching%20describes%20the%20reality%20of,inaccessible%2C%20away%20in%20his%20palace%2C%20distant%20and%20removed.

"Righteousness." Your Dictionary. https://www.yourdictionary.com/righteousness.

Roat, A. "What Is The Tetragrammaton?" https://www.christianity.com/wiki/christian-terms/what-is-the-tetragrammaton-meaning-and-usage.html.

"Sacrifice." Lexico Online Dictionary. https://www.lexico.com/definition/sacrifice

"Sarah: The Mother of the Jewish Nation." Women in the Bible, 2020. Sarah – The Mother of the Jewish Nation | Women in the Bible (womeninscripture.com).

"Sarai." Babynamepedia. https://www.babynamespedia.com/meaning/Sarai.

"Shavonne." Think Baby Names, 2021. Shavonne - Name Meaning, What does Shavonne mean? (thinkbabynames.com).

"Simon." Think Baby Names, 2021. Simon - Name Meaning, What does Simon mean? (thinkbabynames.com).

Soelaiman, Tubagus. "Geothermal energy." https://www.sciencedirect.com/topics/engineering/hot-dry-rock.

"Spiritus." Latin Dictionary. http://latindictionary.wikidot.com/noun:spiritus.

Sproul, R.C. "The Will of God," https://www.monergism.com/thethreshold/articles/onsite/wills_sproul.html

"The Beautiful Names in Hebrew, " The Beautiful Names of Allah. https://wahiduddin.net/words/99_pages/app_d_hebrew.htm.

"The Hebrew Meaning of "Jesus." Hebrew Streams. http://www.hebrew-streams.org/frontstuff/jesus-yeshua.html.

"The History of the American Flag." PBS. https://www.pbs.org/a-capitol-fourth/history/old-glory/#:~:text=The%20stripes%20represent%20the%20original,represents%20vigilance%2C%20perseverance%20and%20justice.

"The Meaning of Elohim in Hebrew." Hope from the Bible. http://www.hopefromthebible.com/meaning-of-elohim-in-hebrew#:~:text=The%20root%20word%20of%20%22Elohim%22%20is%20%22El%2C%22%20and,authority%2C%22%20or%20%22a%20strong%20one%20with%20great%20authority.%22

"The Meaning of 'El Shaddai." Knowing the Bible. The Meaning of El Shaddai (knowingthebible.net).

"The name of God: What 'Ehyeh asher Ehyeh' means," The Church without Walls. https://churchwithoutwallsinternational.org/2019/02/15/the-name-of-god-what-ehyeh-asher-ehyeh-means-1/.

"The Verb to be," Linguapress. https://linguapress.com/grammar/to-be.htm#:~:text=The%20verb%20to%20be%20is%20used%20as%20an,followed%20by%20the%20present%20participle%20of%20a%20verb.

"To give up the ghost: to breathe one's last breath." Word History. https://wordhistories.net/2018/06/18/give-ghost-die/#:~:text=The%20phrase%20to%20give%20up,as%20the%20principle%20of%20life.

"Torso." Vocabulary. https://www.vocabulary.com/dictionary/torso.

Bibliography

Warch, Bill. 2019. "The Little-Known Purpose of the Cornerstone". https://www.billwarch.com/blog/the-little-known-purpose-of-the-cornerstone/.

"What does the Hebrew word ruach mean?" Compelling Truth. https://www.compellingtruth.org/meaning-ruach.html#:~:text=When%20coupled%20with%20one%20of%20the%20names%20of,%22Spirit%20of%20the%20Lord%22%20or%20%22Spirit%20of%20God.%22.

"What does the name Jesus mean?" Jesus Film Project. https://www.jesusfilm.org/blog-and-stories/jesus-name-mean.html.

"What is the meaning of Adonai?" Compelling Truth. https://www.compellingtruth.org/meaning-of-Adonai.html#:~:text=Adonai%20is%20a%20form%20of%20the%20word%20adon%2C,Kings%206%3A5%29%2C%20and%20even%20oldest%20brothers%20%28Genesis%2032%3A4%29.

"What Is The Tetragrammaton? The unpronounceable four-letter name of God." My Jewish Learning. https://www.myjewishlearning.com/article/the-tetragrammaton/.

White, James. 1986. "Prototokos ("Firstborn"): Its Meaning and Usage In the New Testament." https://www.aomin.org/aoblog/general-apologetics/prototokos-firstborn-its-meaning-and-usage-in-the-new-testament/.

Williams, Michael. "How Does the Bible Define Righteousness?" https://www.whatchristianswanttoknow.com/how-does-the-bible-define-righteousness/.

Wilson, Jared. "What Is the Apostles' Creed?" https://www.christianity.com/theology/the-apostles-creed-part-one-introduction.html.

"Why is Elohim plural?". Rightly Dividing the Word of the Truth. https://rightwordtruth.com/why-is-elohim-plural/#:~:text=%E2%80%9CElohim%E2%80%9D%20is%20plural%20for%20%E2%80%9CEl%E2%80%9D.%20Many%20believe%20that,passage%20records%20Jacob%E2%80%99s%20physical%20struggle%20with%20%E2%80%9Ca%20Man%E2%80%9D.

www.ingramcontent.com/pod-product-compliance
Lightning Source LLC
Chambersburg PA
CBHW071433160426
43195CB00013B/1883